ACRES
of Life

LESSONS LEARNED
ON A FAMILY DAIRY FARM

Nancy J. (Zander) Kalsow

Editing by Holly Henschen, www.HollyHenschen.com
Book Cover Design by Julie Underwood, www.julieunderwood.tumblr.com

ISBN – 978-1-7342140-0-0
Library of Congress Control Number: 2019918432

Learn more about Nancy's coaching packages and create more joy in your life:
www.KalsowCoach.com

Life is full of rich material to help us learn and grow. Nancy has taken this a step farther by capturing special memories from growing up on her family farm so that readers can not only enjoy reliving these rich moments with her, but also learn with her. Whether you've spent any time on a farm or not, Nancy's writing will immerse you in the experience so you can understand and appreciate the life lessons she shares. Her wisdom and insights are designed to help you find joy, love, and resilience in your own life.

—Tina Hallis, Ph.D., Author of Sharpen Your Positive Edge

In her new book, Acres of Life, *Nancy Zander Kalsow, with careful research and skilled use of language, describes the life she lived as a little girl and young woman growing up on a southern Wisconsin dairy farm in the 1960s and 1970s. She shares the good and the bad, the fun and the sad. She writes about the long days of summer work and the challenging days of winter, all a part of her growing up years. Reflecting on those days, she identifies several of what she calls "powerful life lessons." Lots to be learned from reading this book.*

—Jerry Apps, Author of *Simple Things: Lessons From The Family Farm*

A good read about the trials, tribulations, and triumphs of a family's life on a southern Wisconsin dairy farm.

—Andrew Faust, Retired CEO of Summit Credit Union

Acres of Life *took me back to my childhood when life was beautifully simple, carefree, and filled with many of the same lessons Nancy shares in her book. It made me appreciate growing up in rural Wisconsin more than ever! Reading her book spoke to me in so many ways and confirmed why I teach and continue to share many of these valuable lessons with my second graders.* Acres of Life *is a book that everyone should read! Nancy allows the reader to fully experience the joys of life in a rural community and the "lifelong" lessons to pass on to the next generation.*

—**Jamie Mawhinney,** Second Grade Teacher, Madison Metropolitan School District

Dedication

To my parents, Charleen C. Zander and
the late Kenneth F. Zander,
for instilling the virtues of love and respect.

To my siblings, for making this life an adventure
through the shared experiences
reflected in many of the life lessons
entwined in these pages.

Table of Contents

INTRODUCTION

Growing up Zander

I believe experience is the best teacher in life. Mistakes build character. New situations awaken the senses and manifest growth. Moments of sadness, or pain in life—they are the impetus to appreciate the opposite rise of elation that comes in times of happiness.

We all have our own experiences we learn from, but we also have the amazing ability to learn from others through their stories; stories of their adventures, their loss, their decisions, their learnings. By sharing our stories, we can relive and reflect on moments and bring clarity to our future. This book is an invitation for you to step into my story so that you might recall your own past lessons and maybe even define some new ones.

My story is not flashy or mysterious. I'm just a normal girl who is proud to say I grew up on a family dairy farm in rural Wisconsin. Believe me, I was not always proud of that. Life on a dairy farm in the 1960s and 1970s was not glamourous. I hated the stench. I was embarrassed by the outdated hand-me-downs I wore. The physical work was hard. I despised the stigma. I missed out on taking vacations or hanging out with my friends. I wanted to go shopping on weekends, not bale hay and milk cows. There were a lot of responsibilities running a 24-hours-a day, 7-days-a-week family business. Responsibility coupled with physical labor create the perfect environment for learning. The result: a lot of practical life lessons. Some tough, some happy, some painful.

This book began as a project for my family. A legacy of sorts. I had planned to document some family history, our plight and our kinship, for future generations of Zanders. In the process of doing that, it became clear to me that what I had experienced as I grew up on this farm provided powerful life lessons. By writing my experiences, I uncovered some secrets as to why I make decisions and why I react to situations the way I do today. It's helped me to lead a genuinely happy life as I connect more deeply to who I truly am. It's also helped me respect and accept others for who they are.

◆ ◆ ◆

ACRE 1

True Love

B eer schlobber and waitress. That's how it all began. With Charleen looking all cute in her pink polka dot dress, a fancy lace apron, and special pink gloves. She was excited to help serve the meal at her Aunt Laura and Uncle Jake's 25th wedding anniversary luncheon. It was a special day. All the relatives had come to celebrate and neighbors, too. The party took place in the valley on Moen Valley Road. And, in traditional German style, there was beer. It began with Kenneth going from table to table, pouring beer into the glasses of relatives and friends. His cousin, Jake, celebrating his 25th wedding anniversary to Charleen's Aunt Laura. FATE.

Although they had only lived two miles from each other their entire lives, nearly 20 years, Kenneth F. Zander and Charleen C. Brunner had never met until that day. Charleen, just 17, had attended Edgewood High School in Madison—very prestigious for a local farm girl. The daughter of Leo and Hilda Brunner lived right outside of Cross Plains on then Highway 14, which later became County Road KP. Kenneth, age 19, was a local farmer, the son of Charles and Theresa Zander, operating his family farm on the corner of the same Highway 14 and Moen Valley Road.

After the meal, in typical fashion, the men played cards and the women cleaned up the mess! Kenneth kept his eye on Charleen. He probably lost a hand or two of the Euchre games due to his roaming eyes. Charleen caught him looking at her and felt embarrassed. Kenneth quickly turned away and avoided eye contact when Charleen noticed him. Flirting at its best. Charleen was very charming. How can one be anything but charming in a pink polka dot dress? After nearly two hours of pretending to not notice one another, Kenneth was finally brave enough to ask Charleen for a date. Little did they know that this celebration of marriage would lead to another.

They had just gotten to know each other when news traveled quickly through the valley of a farm accident. News like this always came with prayers for the injured and support for the family involved. It was a beautiful fall day, September 20, 1950, and fall corn harvesting had just begun. After working the land for five months, from prepping to planting and cultivating, harvesting was a farmer's pride. Weather factors were watched closely at the various stages of growth—too much rain and the crop would be lost; not enough and the crop would also be lost.   In God's hands—as it was every year. The 1950 crop was healthy. Thick corn stalks make for warm cow bedding in the cold winter months ahead and the large corn cobs of corn produce plenty of silage to fill the silo and keep the stock fed well throughout the winter months when no grass can be found. The corn was at its prime. Row after row awaiting the machine to take it in, separating the stalk from the cob and ejecting them—stalks on the ground to be chopped for bedding and cobs into the bin in the back of the machine to be ground into silage later.

Farm machinery required regular maintenance and often broke down in the middle of its job, calling for the farmer to be skilled in mechanical repair of all sorts. On this day, those thick stalks clogged the chutes to the auger and the machine instantly stalled. The young, healthy farmer was strong and skilled at common outages such as this. He left the tractor running idle, jumped off the tractor seat, and climbed down to inspect the situation. When the farmer reached in to pull the fibrous stalks out, his glove got caught as the machine went back to work. The machine had no mercy. It did not recognize the fingers and forearm it had sucked into the same channel as the cornstalks. It did not stop until it was stuck again; this time with flesh and bone. Thankfully, Kenneth could be heard shouting for help by his sister, who happened to be home from college and out picking berries.

The ambulance was called and arrived from Madison nearly 30 minutes later. Kenneth had lost quite a bit of blood, although pressure had been placed on the wound. Several pieces of his right arm were collected and sent with him. Unfortunately, it could not be re-attached—his right arm had been mutilated to the point of no repair.

Charleen was arriving home from her job at Manufactured Batteries Inc., where she typed out numbers through carbon paper to keep track of the inventory and sales for the manufacturer of batteries. The ambulance had just picked up its passenger and went roaring past. She prayed for whoever was inside. When she returned to her home farm, her mother was just hanging up the phone. She had been interrupted on the phone line shared by neighbors in rural areas referred to as a 'party line.' Charleen's mother shared, "It's been a terrible day—terrible day." The Theis boy, Dave, had fallen and suffered a concussion and Kenneth Zander had lost his arm.

St. Mary's Hospital in downtown Madison was Kenneth's home for the next eight days. He was bandaged and on pain-numbing medication. After several days, he began the grueling therapy to heal the physical and mental scars associated with the loss of a limb. He strengthened the remaining nub of his upper arm and pushed through the throbbing bandage changes. He struggled with accepting his one-armed body. He mourned the loss of his dominant hand. Even though he was in pain, he slept soundly. Farmers are known to do that whenever they have the opportunity. He became known as quite the charmer with the nurses. One day, while he slept, the nurses painted his toenails, much to his dismay. He enjoyed teasing them in return, winking and giving them reason to remain at his beck and call. That was my dad, long before he became my dad—everyone loved him. He had a sparkle in his eyes and could address anyone by their name with a personalized ring to it, making you feel special. More importantly, he believed you were.

Kenneth's cousin, Ronnie Zander, drove Charleen to the hospital to see Kenneth the first time during his eight-day stay. He was happy to see her and asked her to come back to see him again. And so she did. Her parents were going to visit a neighbor who had just had a baby and she tagged along. She snuck into Ken's room and planted a nice slobbery kiss on his lips to wake him up. When he opened his eyes, they lit up like a sparkler. Today, my mother insists she can't recall a lot of details about these visits. She is either forgetful or elusive—I believe it to be the latter.

After several weeks of recovery, the neighbors held a benefit for Kenneth. A fundraising dance to help cover medical costs and a new arm. A few rolling hills and another valley over was the town of Springfield Corners and a local dance hall. Charleen's first cousin, Ruth Brunner-Maier, picked her up and off they went to the benefit. Ruth suspected some chemistry between her cousin and the now one-handed farmer and so, she left Charleen to fend for herself. Charleen, while waiting for a request to dance, sipped on some punch. Sure enough, Kenneth finally got up the courage to ask for that dance. He wrapped his remaining arm behind her back and together they swayed to the music. He took Charleen home and they officially began dating.

Kenneth accepted his fate and knew he had to get back to work. Farming was not easy with one arm and so, he took a stab at selling insurance. After just a few weeks, his father suffered a heart attack and Ken knew his mother would need him to keep the farm afloat. He was bound and determined to keep farming, even though some thought it was impossible to do with only one arm.

Life Lesson: Hold tight to your dream. Where there is a will, there's a way.

His sister and brother-in-law lived in Minneapolis at the time—home of the Trautman artificial limb company. Kenneth acquired his first prosthetic arm before the end of 1950. He tried several options, but the metal 'Captain Hook' was always his preferred limb. It provided the strength for working with tough farm equipment and could tolerate getting smashed by a hammer or the frost of the cold winter—with no frostbite! Learning to work the muscles of his "phantom arm" was no treat. Just opening and closing the hook took practice and, along with it, his share of frustrations. The hook was handy for large motor skills and made a fine tool to place the handle of a five-gallon pail or handle of a shovel. It took him over a year to master the fine motor skills. Although he could tie his shoes with one hand, he did decide that loafers were the way to go with most shoes. Except the shit kickers for farm work—these above the ankle boots were pre-laced and tied so that he was able to tighten them with one hand. He stuck with his dream of running a dairy operation, along with chickens, hogs, beef, and over 160 acres of fieldwork.

My parents dated throughout these trials and tribulations as my dad adjusted to his new life with one less limb. Favorite date destinations included picnics, county fairs, and the drive-in movie theater —after evening milking, of course.

On a warm August day in 1951, they were off on a date to the Wisconsin State Fair—a quick day trip between morning and evening milking sessions. Kenneth's mom had sent some items along for him to drop off at his brother's farm in Deerfield. After driving down the driveway to Raymond's house, Kenneth appeared a bit nervous. They quickly dropped off the items and departed back towards the main road. As they arrived at the top of knoll near the end of the driveway, Ken put the car in park, turned to Charleen and popped the question. She said YES! Kenneth seemed surprised. When she asked why, he said "Because I only have one arm and I'm not sure if I deserve you." She responded with, "I'm not marrying your arm—I'm marrying you!" From that day forward, the arm was a symbol of survival, of hope, of courage, of love, and of acceptance.

Life Lesson: Find the courage to accept one another just the way you are.

Sept. 1950 BLACK EARTH

KENNETH ZANDER, 20, LOSES RIGHT ARM

Kenneth Zander, 20, son of Mr. and Mrs. Charles Zander lost his right arm about six inches below the shoulder Monday. He was cleaning a corn chopper and as he reached for a stalk his hand became caught in the gears and was drawn into the machine. He was alone in the field at the time but his call for help was heard by the men at the barn who responded promptly. He was taken to St. Mary's hospital, where the mangled arm was amputated.

At last reports he is getting along as well as can be expected but is suffering a lot of pain as can be expected.

On May 28, 1952, they were married at St. Francis Xavier Church in Cross Plains. My parents' love grew without pomp and circumstance. There were no splendid displays of romance—it was simple affection every day. A look, a smile, a brush of the hand. They worked hard to build a life and a family.

I do not recall my parents 'fighting' or even being frustrated with one another. I'm sure they were— but, in the end, they believed in each other and their love for one another. You'll see this demonstrated throughout the chapters of this book.

Love is patient and kind; love does not envy or boast; it is not arrogant or rude. It does not insist on its own way; it is not irritable or resentful; It does not rejoice at wrong-doing. But rejoices with the truth. Love bears all things (ALL things), *believes all things, hopes all things, endures all things.*
—1 Corinthians 13:4-7

Charleen and Ken Zander - 35th Anniversary

My parents went through 55 years of marriage holding true to that passage from the Bible. It is recited at many wedding ceremonies, yet it is hard to live by. We are human.

My mom and dad had their own share of obstacles and challenges. They endured, fought through, and conquered each one. When they disagreed, they learned to let go and move on. A lasting grudge is irrational—learn to let go. True love means respect for one another, accepting one another, thanking one another, encouraging one another. My parents are the epitome of true love.

Life Lesson: Respect, accept and encourage one another.

◆ ◆ ◆

ACRE 2

The Zander Clan-
Tales of sibling rivalry
and bonding

I am #7. The seventh child born to Kenneth Francis Zander and Charleen Catherine (Brunner) Zander. The youngest girl, but not the baby. Over the span of 15 years, my mother gave birth nine times. Nine times! Even more audacious was the fact that along with nine kids comes the cooking, cleaning, gardening, canning, lack of sleep, and, oh yeah, laundry. Without the modern conveniences, my mom used an old wringer washing machine for loads and loads of laundry, including all the cloth diapers necessary for our brood.

1. Terry 2. Linda 3. Joyce 4. Sharon 5. Steven 6. Cathy 7. Nancy 8. Scott 9. Alan

The Good Lord called #8 home after only two days. Born a 'blue baby,' he was held and loved by my mother as he struggled from lack of oxygen. I was three years and one month old when Scott Allen was born, so I don't remember how painful it was. I do remember the house being quite solemn. I do remember standing at the living room window overlooking our wide driveway and watching my Grandma Brunner march to the house to help take care of the rest of us. My Grandma Brunner was a farm wife herself and had raised five children of her own. She was serious and stoic. Stepping in to help was not much fun for her. There were seven of us and she had done her fair share already. The day Scott Allen went to heaven, my Grandma Brunner picked my siblings up from school. She shared how well Mom was doing and that she would get to come home in a few days. My sister, Sharon, only nine years old at the time, asked, "How's the baby?" The answer was simply, "He died." My dad and two of my siblings attended the small burial in the St. Francis Xavier Cemetery where Scott's name was added to the tombstone of my grandparents. He joined Charles H. Zander and the then open-ended 'dash' for Theresa Zander.

My mom was still healing and could not attend the burial, neither emotionally nor physically. On the inside, she was at odds with the disdain and torment of losing her own flesh and blood. But, there was little time to mourn. Today, I admire her for pushing through as she continued the routine onslaught of tasks necessary to keep our large family growing in health and faith. As a mother myself, it is difficult for me to think about the sorrow and pain she experienced. She taught me resilience.

Life Lesson: Resilience—push through and carry on.

Alan Craig Zander

Almost exactly two years after Scott passed, my baby brother, Alan, was born. I was five and had no idea what I was in for. My older siblings, however, had been through this before. Or had they? For the first five months of his life, my mom and the doctors had a hard time figuring out what Alan could eat. His stomach could not tolerate the traditional baby formulas, whether dairy, soy, rice, or others. He was tiny and having a hard time growing from lack of nutrients. I'm sure this was scary for my mom, who was still a bit raw from the loss of Scott. After trying a variety of concoctions, it seemed that the stinky meat-based milk was our one and only option. He sucked cheerfully on that bottle nipple while the rest of us literally plugged our noses! He did start to grow, and I was allowed to hold him and help tend to his needs. I learned, the hard way, to 'cover up' when you change the diaper of a baby boy. I was thrilled to have a baby to take care of since I was not in school full days yet.

One day, around the age of two, Alan began screaming uncontrollably in pain. Even the touch of a diaper on his belly sent him wailing. Back for another doctor's visit, he was diagnosed with a ruptured appendix and taken into emergency surgery. For days, we waited and prayed and prayed and waited. A ruptured appendix meant bacteria had leaked into his entire body. It held a "highly likely" death rate in the '60s. Since we shared a house with my grandmother, we'd gather around her kitchen table. She would lead us in prayer, asking the Good Lord to let this one survive. Eventually, we got the news that he would. Little Alan came home with a massive scar. His entire belly sliced open and cleaned out.

Life Lesson: Prayer is powerful.

Alan's recovery from appendicitis was difficult as the incision oozed and drained. The six-inch incision on this two-year-old required frequent dressing changes to avoid infection. Two years old and over half of his tummy had been cut open. Eventually it healed, and Alan required a little less attention. However, he continued to have many trips to the emergency room over the next two years due to frequent and lengthy nosebleeds. I remember my sisters rocking him and pinching his nose shut for hours until, inevitably, Mom and Dad would take him to the hospital for the painful procedure of cauterization each time. Alan needed and received a lot of tender loving care from his family. As things settled down and he had less of our attention, he began to grow a temper. Then, he became rotten! Figuratively, of course. He ate fresh rendered lard right out of the bucket and wiped it on my Mom's church dress. He'd get angry and lay on his tummy and pound his fists on the floor because it had tripped him. "You dumb floor! You tripped me, stupid floor!" he'd pound and rant for several minutes. We often played together in the front yard, but this was not without confrontation of its own kind. Sharing a tire swing or the large tractor innertube trampoline often meant a roust. I usually would end up hopping on my bike, but even that could not remove me from his wrath of aggressive jealousy. As I rode past him, he swung a croquet mallet and struck me in the head. He was a naughty boy. Alan fought over where he got to sit, what he got to do, and when he got to do it. Nancy gave in. Until . . . the fight over the cow cushion—a large footstool Cathy, Alan, and I shared in my grandma's living room. He crossed the line when he wanted the "middle" of the cushion and I wouldn't move. His clawed hands reached up to my biceps, fingers dug in deep, and he pulled those sharp little fingernails all the way down my arm. I went crying to Mom and my sister followed. Once comforted, Cathy turned to me and said, "Why don't you scratch him back? If you don't defend yourself, he is going to keep on doing it." Wise words. I had been so worried that I would hurt him after all he had been through and now, I heard it was ok to fight back.

Life Lesson: Fight back—learn to stand up for yourself.

Catherine Ann Zander

Just three years older than me, I learned to trust

her and, therefore, she brought out the 'gullible' in me. I always believed her. From being able to see the men walking on the moon during that "giant leap for mankind" to the glowing red truck cigarette lighter being safe to touch! "Go ahead, put your finger on it, it's not hot." When she could smell the sizzling flesh and heard a scream from me, she mustered, "I guess maybe it is hot" with a snicker.

Yet, she and I managed to be friends. We shared a bedroom and, on the hot summer nights, would lay with our heads at the feet-end so that we could feel the warm breeze from the window box fan. We would talk and laugh late into the night. Sometimes so hard and so long that we would inevitably hear the stomp of our mother's footsteps down the long hallway. "You two settle down, it's late," she'd say. Cathy and I would literally hold our breath until she got to the other end of the hall, and then we'd burst into laughter again. Seconds later, Mom was back to remind us how late it was. In the winter, we would build snow forts and run across the top of the snow mounds made from the plowed driveway, playing Batman and Robin. It didn't dawn on me for several years that she was always Batman! Years later, I reminded her that behind every superhero is a wise sidekick.

Cathy was the one who taught me how to drive. Taking me to the back field, she would have me maneuver through made-up scenarios. My favorite was when she shouted, "Look out for that dog!" making me slam on the brakes. I'm not sure which one of us was more surprised by my quick reaction and our stiff necks. When I came down with allergies that induced asthma, she insisted I was faking it. "You just want to get out of the chores," she'd say as I wheezed and tried to catch my breath while forking the dusty cow bedding into the barn stanchions. Cathy liked the farm work more than any of the rest of us combined. Her tomboy nature led to adventures and more accidents than the rest of us, too. When she was three, she jumped over a hot vaporizer and burned herself. She attended my baptism swaddled in a blanket smothered with soothing salve. At five, she fell through thin ice on the ditch, which resulted in rheumatic fever, an inflammatory disease that can develop as a complication of inadequately treated strep throat or scarlet fever. The rheumatic fever meant monthly trips for the next 13 years to the Dean Clinic on Fish Hatchery Road in Madison for a penicillin shot in the butt. We learned to appreciate these trips as they often involved a stop at Treasure Island, a discount store. It was a favorite place to shop for clothes, school supplies, and 'treasures' like the owl-shaped macramé plant holder that hung in my bedroom all through high school.

Cathy was strong and confident. She was not afraid to jump down hay chutes or off the garage roof. We both temporarily lost our hearing when she got ahold of some firecrackers and lit the whole pack, which exploded in her hand. The ringing in our ears had us too scared to tell our mother. At one point, my older siblings had nicknamed Cathy "Chink" because she happened to walk into the room while they were describing the swaying hips of their school teacher's walk. *Chink-a-boom, chink-a-boom.* She laughed and accepted the name in fun. As you can imagine it was not the best name to be using while we were out in public, and yet we did. For years, we referred to her as "Chink."

We all got to choose one sport and basketball was hers. Cathy played hard, fought for the ball, and drove to the basket. She was well liked and a basketball star. All 5' 2" of her navigated the court. I loved watching her play the year I was a freshman in high school and she, a senior. The next fall, I stood in the garage watching her back the car out, heading to the University of Wisconsin–LaCrosse for college. I bravely waved goodbye and ran to my bedroom and bawled. My best friend had just left.

Life Lesson: My sisters will be forever friends.

Steven Leo Zander

Five years my senior. I remember him reading comic books and usually working on putting something back together. He didn't hang with me much until I was about six years old. Then Steven, Cathy, and I were a threesome. We played under an old flatbed wagon that was parked next to the chicken coop. Someone had dug a four-feet-deep pit underneath and we could stand up under there. We used Mom's old vinyl kitchen table cloths to cover the dirt, oftentimes mud, that had washed down the sides of the pit. We sat on an old toilet seat, which we stole from the family outhouse, as our chair. We stored treasures in the axle of the wagon and a few comic books found their way in, too. It was here we spoke Pig Latin or other made up languages and this carried over to our time doing chores in the barn. Steven is the one who taught me the 'gutter skip,' a game we played to entertain ourselves in between washing the cow udders and switching the milk machines from cow to cow. It was a game of footwork skill and the winner was determined by the highest count of skip-kicks from side to side in the gutter without falling in the manure. Fun times! Steven was also the inventor of our spy and bomb kits. We used anything we could find in the barn as make-believe 'explosives' that we'd plant in various 'targets' around the farm as part of our missions. From barn lime to sileage, ground corn, and little pieces of dry hay. We'd spend hours writing secret codes on tiny scrolls of paper and band them with our sister Sharon's orthodontic rubber bands. The scrolls communicated where we would meet up and tactics for our missions. These scrolls were stored in round makeup powder compacts after my mother had emptied them. They fit nicely in a pocket or shoe for safe and secret storage.

Life Lesson: Imagination is better than any toy you can purchase.

As he got older, the farm felt more stifling to Steve, and he could not wait to move out. He began argu-

ing with my dad and it was one of the few times I remember my dad being angry with anyone. Steve was
convinced the Navy was his calling and, at age 17, he
asked a military recruiter to come and get my dad
to give his permission. Dad calmly stated, "The Navy
seems like a great place and when you are 18, you
will be old enough to make that decision yourself."
Steve was not happy. The day after Steve turned 18,
my dad gave him a choice to stay and work on the
farm, leave, or stay and pay rent. Steve left and stayed
with friends for a while. But then, he actually did it!
He joined the Navy and worked hard to graduate from
the academy. You see, in the Navy, it turns out you *do*
need to know how to swim! Steve did not. The ser-
geant split the group into swimmers and non-swim-
mers. After some quick lessons, the testing began—
jumping into the ocean, treading water, and a lengthy
back float. He failed the first two times. He had one
more chance to succeed. I'm sure he wanted to prove
to my dad that he had made the right choice. Steve
persevered, and my parents took a rare vacation to
San Diego to see him graduate. I admired him for following his dream. There is nothing like seeing a sailor
in full dress. Especially when it is your brother. Eventually, he became certified in submarine and nuclear
energy. He spent months at sea, deep in the ocean. His
visits home were rare and brought the excitement of
stories from his travels. One of my favorite memories
is the trip home he happened to make when I turned
16. He brought me a heart-shaped charm for my
bracelet that said "Sweet 16" on it. Today, this charm

is a treasure of mine.

Life Lesson: Your decisions. Your Outcomes. Choose wisely.

Sharon Kay Zander

She was teased by her older sisters and was too old to hang out with the younger ones. She begged my mom to stay home from school to take care of me as a baby. I have no recollection of Sharon until she was an awkward lanky teenager. She had hair longer than her legs and crooked teeth that were behind metal braces for over five years. We share the characteristics of the long Zander nose, with a bump between nostrils and forehead, and were both teased because of it. Sharon was the middle sister. She felt alone and left out. She liked to read and could often be found curled up with a good book away from the rest of us. She regularly became the scapegoat for her older sisters' shenanigans, but never did she guess her baby brother would do such a thing to her. Once, while she was curled up in a chair around the corner from where Alan was playing, he blurted out a few choice words. From the kitchen, my mom said, "Alan Zander! Where did you learn to swear like that?" He looked up at Sharon, who was out of my mother's sight, and stated, "Share On!" I'm confident Mom did not fall for that one.

Sonny and Cher Bono were a big musical hit with a weekly television show in the '70s. I thought it was pretty cool that Sharon looked like Cher Bono with her long hair, long nose and now-straight teeth. Then, she even started hanging out with a handsome guy with a mustache who looked like Sonny. Her boy-friend, now husband, Dan, respected my dad and en-joyed discussions with him. That was pretty cool, too. Dan insisted that Sharon move away from home and live on her own before he would marry her. She did. I was devastated when they got married and I was the only sister not in the wedding. Life goes on, and Sharon became my soul sister. As I grew older, I recog-nized the similarities in our personalities, as well as our facial features. When I was a senior in high school, I had the privilege of helping her take care of her first child. Sharon was a nervous mom and I was dreaming of opening my own daycare, so off I went to take care of this sweet little day-old baby girl.

Life Lesson: Don't let a disappointment or disagree-ment get in the way of a relationship.

Today, many say Sharon and I are the most alike. It's true. We look the same, laugh the same, and we are both gentle souls. Sensitive and naïve, the two of us together could take on the burden of worry for the entire family. I may have been too little to be her tag-a-long as a child, but that did not stop me as an adult. She secured a job at State Capitol Employ-ees Credit Union right after high school. In 1984, I was asked to join them because of Sharon's hard work ethic. At work, many were confused by our voices and which one of us they were talking to on the phone. Even her own daughters had a hard time tell-ing Sharon and me apart, especially our voices. One day, Sharon left a message on her family's home phone with some chores she wanted her daughters to do. When she came home from work, they told her about this strange message Aunt Nancy had left for them. Confused, they all crowded around the answering machine and burst into laughter when they realized it was their own mother and not Aunt Nancy. I was honored.

My three oldest siblings, Terry, Linda, and Joyce, were born almost exactly one year apart from each other. They were often described as a unit. They were the ones who grew up inside a playpen in the barn while Mom and Dad kept the farm running. They were the ones who made the local paper, sitting on the milk cooler in their new, modern, sanitary milk house in 1956. They were the ones who attended Catholic school, and they were the ones that had to take care of the 'little ones.' I was little, and, I'm sure, 'in the way' of the older siblings. Because of my age difference with these now-teenagers, I was often left out of things—especially inside jokes. When I walked into a room, I was sure they were talking about me. They looked my way with peering eyes and whispered. I often felt intimidated and shy. I wondered if I was good enough; my confidence wavered. In retrospect, I'm sure they were protecting my sensitive ears from words I was too young to hear or understand!

Life Lesson: It's none of your business what others think of you! And almost always, it's not about you.

Terrence Kenneth Zander

The first-born child. A son might be one of the best things that can happen to a farmer. I imagine him to be a well-received gift. My parents were just young farmers at ages 23 and 21, trying to make ends meet. A son was a farmer's pride in knowing the family tradition might be carried on, and Terry did not disappoint. He was a good big brother, but preferred to be with his dad versus his sisters. He liked to follow in his dad's footsteps and tagged along to help with many farm chores. He was 10 when I was born, and I don't recall much about him until he was practically a grown man. At age 15, he would lie on his stomach in front of the TV and laugh at a variety of comedy shows or follow the stories in old Western movies. I sometimes sat on his back to watch along with him. I remember how his laughter had me bouncing around, making me laugh along with him.

He passed his driver's license road test and was a typical teenager who wanted to cruise in his hard-earned red Chevy Malibu. He enjoyed hanging out with local farmers and friends and went out many evenings. They enjoyed beer and talking smart. Getting up for morning chores was not in his nature and, therefore, he became a bit lazy for daytime farm duties. The late-night shenanigans eventually caught up with him, and he learned a painful lesson after crashing his car on his way home from one of them. There was a lot of moaning and groaning from his bedroom for a week or so and I'm not sure it was from the cuts and bruises or the fact his car was totaled. Probably a bit of both. He got a girlfriend, and I remember the two of them always having fun together. Arm wrestling, tickling, and lots of giggling. Cheryl became part of our family. Throughout their dating, they took the two little ones—Alan and me—on outings to church picnics and parks. When they married, they lived in the farmhouse across the highway on South Valley Road. Terry continued to farm with my dad and partnered with him to keep the farm running.

Linda Susan Zander

Nine years older than me, she is studious and smart. As the oldest girl, I guess she had something to prove. And she did. She got straight A's, and when I entered high school six years after she graduated, the teachers still asked, "Are you Linda's sister?" Yes, indeed I was, but it was not apparent academically. I held my own, but never could hold a candle to Linda. Linda made household chores more fun by leading us in songs she had learned in church and from her favorite folk group, Peter, Paul and Mary. As we washed and dried dishes, we sang songs like "Puff, the Magic Dragon," "Let There Be Peace On Earth," and "Where Have All The Flowers Gone."

Heading off to college was a tremendous feat for our family, and Ms. Smarty Pants Linda did not let us down. She headed to the University of Wisconsin–La Crosse and graduated *cum laude* with a degree in mathematics, a minor in computer science and a teaching degree. When she came home for visits, Alan was clearly her favorite. He waited for her to drive in, and she'd scoop him up and take care of him like he was her own. After college, she worked for the CIA and was sworn to secrecy. We never heard from her again!

More seriously, she has modeled courage and independence by venturing out into this world. She traveled the country and lived in a variety of states, holding executive-level jobs her entire adult life.

Life Lesson: Venture courageously.

Joyce Marie Zander

Eight years older than me, she was always a busy bee, capable of getting more work done than two of the others of us together. I think it was her way of hustling to get done with the task so that she had time to goof off. The three oldest sisters shared a bedroom. Sharon and Joyce fought about everything, including clothes, space, and looks. They had to share a bed, which brought on hitting and kicking. Joyce would be caught standing in front of the bedroom mirror telling herself how beautiful she was. Sharon gave her a hard time about talking to herself, yet those positive affirmations are probably the reason Joyce is the most comfortable with her body today. They fought over which one of them was loved more by Grandma Zander and each insists that Grandma told them that she liked her cleaning the best. Little did they know that Grandma told each one of us that!

As a high schooler, Joyce became a TROUBLE maker! She dated the hired hands, partied on the Mazomanie countryside, and went to toga and toker (smoker) parties. She was a bit of a rebel and wanted to get away from the nagging constant routine of the farm. She got married the November after she graduated high school and moved out when I was in 6th grade. She became a young mother, and I was thrilled to be asked to babysit and hang out in her home. She was a good homemaker, busy cooking and cleaning and organizing. Even though Joyce was a wild child, she knew, as we all did, that we were always welcome to come back home. Late one night, after dropping me off from babysitting, her car came peeling back into the farm driveway. I remember the fear in her eyes when she handed her 5-year-old daughter to me and raced back into the night to find her husband, who had taken off with their 2-year-old son. I snuggled with Jessica until Joyce returned with Travis. No words were needed. They were safe. Joyce and I became closer after that. It was painful for Joyce to make the decision to divorce her husband, yet humbling to see how quickly our lives can change. Years later, we learned her husband had a mental illness. Still, Joyce made sure he and his family remained a part of his kids' lives.

Life Lesson: Home is where the heart is. You are always welcomed home.

Over the years, Joyce became an antique connoisseur, scouring for the best deals in the county. She furnished her home with her quality finds made from rich wood, worn fabrics, and bubbled, wavy glass. In addition to working a full-time job and raising two kids, she opened her own business on Main Street in Black Earth called The Crafty Collector. She continues to be a busy beaver.

1987
Front L-R Nancy, Terry, Cathy, Linda
Back row: Steve, Joyce, Sharon, Alan

Throughout my childhood, we were reminded of our very own angel, Scott Allen, in subtle ways. My favorite was the silk poinsettias that were placed in the glass pitcher on top of our console TV at Christmas time. Eight red poinsettias and one white one. For my parents 50th wedding anniversary, my sister Cathy found this poem to place in our family scrapbook. It's a great memorial for Scott Allen Zander—our guardian angel.

God's Angels

When God delivers angels
He picks a special few
To guard the cherished infant
He sends with love to you

Rainbows gleam upon the clouds
When such a child arrives
Whose tenderness and beauty
Will change so many lives

When God retrieves an angel
For reasons of His own
His goodness and His mercy
Seem distant and unknown

But paradise is knowing
A child who never grew
Holds tightly to God's fingers
And watches over you

—Author unknown

Death leaves a heartache no one can heal, love leaves a memory no one can steal.
—From a headstone in Ireland

Life Lesson: Believe in angels!

◆ ◆ ◆

Through the Curtain

L ocated in a glorious Wisconsin valley, our farmhouse is surrounded by rolling hills, a babbling creek, farm pastures, and bountiful fields. The closest town, two miles away, is Black Earth. Yes, the name comes from the rich, black dirt that provides prime conditions for fresh produce and green pastures. It's no wonder my great-grandparents chose to build their lives here.

The large two-story farmhouse was typical for local farm families, many of whom happened to be Catholic. It had four bedrooms and a ventilated corn drying room upstairs. Cobs of corn from the fall harvest were hung on hanger racks to dry out and the seeds loosened for planting next spring. The first floor had been beautifully crafted years earlier and still holds the original woodwork, plaster, and wainscoting today. Large dual sliding pocket doors that disappeared into the walls were pulled together to close off rooms in the winter. Radiator heat, serviced by a coal delivery stocked in the basement, provided warmth. Rooms were spacious with high ceilings. The first floor, where guests were received, had a library/parlor, a living room, a dining room, a large wood-burning-stove kitchen, a large walk-through pantry, one bathroom, another bedroom with a large walk-in closet, and a "wash room" for cleaning up the dirt and smells from the farm. My dad grew up in this house. He was the youngest of five. His siblings 'flew the coop' to start their own families. My dad stayed.

After my parents' wedding in 1952, they began farming together with my grandparents, Charles H. and Theresa Zander. The large farmhouse became home for two families. My grandparents on one side and my parents (with eventually all eight of their kids) on the other. The parlor became my mom and dad's kitchen, the library was converted to a dining room and the one bedroom on the first floor was converted to a living room. Upstairs, my grandparents took one of the four bedrooms and my parents, over time, filled the others with children. As the rooms started filling up, the corn drying room was converted to a fifth bedroom and a bathroom with a shower!

I never got to meet my grandpa, who passed away in 1956 at the age of 57 from a heart attack. My grandma became the sole owner of the Zander Family farm as my dad worked the land. My grandma was respectful of my parent's young relationship and growing family. She gave them the freedom to raise their family and run the farm yet, provided them with support as needed. My parents continued to farm jointly with my grandma and, in 1960, my father purchased the property from her on land contract; a written agreement that made my grandma a virtual bank and provided her a steady income from the monthly payments my father made to her. Grandma continued to live on her side of the house.

One piece of floral fabric hung loosely in a doorway to my "Grandma's Side." I only had to run through the curtain to find my grandma's loving arms and warm lap. She was delighted every time she saw me. I snuggled with her, played with her homemade Raggedy Ann and Andy dolls, and took naps on her couch in the afternoons.

My grandma! Right there. My grandma. Every day. Just through the curtain! MY grandma. When I wanted a hug, through the curtain I'd go. When I wanted a cookie, just through the curtain. When I needed a reprieve from my naughty little brother, I'd run through the curtain and hide. *Ahhh . . .* the safety of Grandma's love.

I was lucky in more ways than one. She gave generously of her patience, love, kindness, hugs, and wittiness. I recall standing on a chair pushed up to the kitchen counter waiting for my toast to pop up. "Grandma, what is that brown spot on your cheek?" I asked. "Oh! That's from getting too close to the toaster when I was waiting for my toast," she teased as she referred to the large brown mole. Even her witty side taught lessons. I stayed off the counter and a little further away from the toaster after that!

My siblings and I loved Grandma's Side through the curtain. She gave us the freedom to use our imagination. She was patient as we invaded her limited space and set up our make-believe dentist's office or schoolroom, using a clothes hamper as the clinic reception or teacher's desk. We used nut picks as our dental tools and homemade powdered sugar frosting as our fillings (most likely the root cause of my rotten teeth, along with our well water without fluoride). Grandma's stationery was used as our school notebooks and her two large, black-bound teacher books, copyrighted in 1915, were our text books. We traced the pages of pictures and penmanship over and over again. I traced hearts and made my own valentine cards. The service window between the pantry and her dining room made for a great place to take down orders for our "café" or use as a high-top desk for real life homework. We loved Grandma's Side.

Life Lesson: The best things in life are free: love, hugs, kindness, patience, and imagination.

My grandma often had visitors. People came to get her advice and indulge in her friendship. I might wake from my nap with my grandma sitting next to me and the eyes of 'strangers' watching me open mine. I was shy and would crawl into Grandma's lap and hide. They would continue their adult conversation. In my own time, I'd be sharing some excitement about a doll or toy or loose tooth with them. My Uncle John heard "loose tooth" as a request to pull it out for me. He did the old 'tie-a-string-around-the-tooth-and-a-doorknob trick.' It was all I could do to lie still on the carpet as he calculated the length of the string needed. He opened the closet door and tied the loose string around the door knob. After confirming that the string remained intact on my tooth, he walked back to the door and slammed it quickly. I'm not sure who was the most surprised when my tooth flew across the room and he caught the string in mid-air with my dangling tooth still attached!

On another visit, my Aunt Catherine and Uncle John delivered a large footstool to my grandma. It was handmade in Brazil from Holstein cowhide—the same breed of cows we milked. A large, black-and-white-spotted piece of cowhide for the top, stitched into eight cowhide panels with sinew string and a bottom piece of solid suede leather. This became known as the "cow cushion" amongst my siblings. It was large enough for at least three of us (and at times four) to sit on and watch soap operas or cartoons with my grandma. We often fought over the exact spot. In current times, we fight over the fact that I have acquired the cow cushion! It lives in my basement awaiting my own grandchildren to share it one day.

My cousins loved to visit the farm and their grandma. Grandma was the common thread and the reason for their visits. They would come to experience the warmth of her kitchen, hugs, and cookies. We would enlist their help with the farm chores, which were exciting to them compared to their 'city' life. After the evening chores, we'd gather around Grandma's large oak table for a late-night game of group Solitaire. Competition and camaraderie ran deep, and so did my Grandma's cookie jar, filled with homemade ginger snaps.

I found warmth in having my grandma through the curtain. From her hugs, sharing a cookie, and through these family visits.

Life Lesson: Find what warms your heart.

My grandma's most frequent visitors were the grandchildren who lived closest to her, just through the curtain. We were never treated as a bother and always welcomed. When my siblings or I were missing, my mom knew where to find us. We hung out with Grandma to watch some of her favorite shows, like *The Honeymooners*, *The Ed Sullivan Show,* and *As the World Turns*. We snuck through the curtain to get out of chores or to stay up past bedtime. We would hide beyond the archway entrance to her kitchen. In the line-of-sight to the television, but far enough into the kitchen where my mom couldn't see us when she poked her head through the curtain to say goodnight to Grandma. Sometimes we got away with it. Oh, how I loved that curtain and everything it represented!

Saturdays were house cleaning days by rotation. Every 5 weeks or so, one of us would get our turn on Grandma's Side. It was the desired location because, after dusting, vacuuming, dishes, and whatever other jobs Grandma had, we'd be rewarded with a coin or two. Maybe even a dollar. But more importantly, we got to see Grandma's things up close. Her books in the long wardrobe with glass doors on each end. Her heirlooms in the built-in china hutch in the dining room, including the pink Depression-era glass, generations of family china and serving bowls, and even a few pieces of jewelry.

A long walk-in closet held other treasures. She had everything in its place and a place for everything, from her fur coat used for warmth, not fashion, to her box of letters from family and friends. Immediately inside the door was a large shelving unit. On the second shelf from the top was an aluminum mug engraved with a floral medallion, filled with old coins from the late 1800s early 1900s. It was a reminder of harder times. The coins that my grandparents used only in an emergency. The coins my siblings and I counted and carefully placed back on the shelf as a reminder to save for hardships.

Life Lesson: Save for what is needed and wait for what is wanted.

In the early '70s, my grandma became weaker and needed more care. My mom was there. From meal prep to bathing, my mom stepped in. My mom was like a superhero. Over the years, she had milked cows with one baby on her hip and another in the playpen. My mom, who laundered cloth diapers for over 16 years. My mom, who gardened, collected eggs, baked bread, and cooked meals. My mom, who stripped and re-sealed cabinets, painted walls, or shampooed carpets after we were all in bed at night. It was my mom who made sure my grandma could stay in her home as long as possible.

In late 1973, my Aunt Mary Lou suggested a nursing home in Thorp, Wisconsin, the town where she and her family resided. She felt it her duty to take care of her mother. The day Grandma moved out was hard on all of us. The curtain remained in place, but it was quiet and lonely when we walked through it. There was no more running through the curtain in the same way ever again. Grandma died in August 1974 at the age of 76. I was not quite 11 years old. Life is short. *Ich liebe dich, Oma!* I love you, Grandma!

Life Lesson: We come into this world with family and leave the world with family. Take care of family.

◆ ◆ ◆

School's out for SUMMER!

Ahhhh! The carefree days of summer. With the sun rising earlier and setting later, my siblings and I were able to enjoy moments, sometimes hours, of free time.

As a youngster, the days were filled playing in the marvelous Wisconsin outdoors, running, skipping, and jumping. The farmyard was large and offered numerous hidden locations to while away the days with our creative minds. The clubhouse converted from an old chicken coop was a favorite secret spot. It had been replaced by a larger, longer, metal chicken coop where we still collected eggs. The clubhouse was tucked behind a small barnwood garage where we stored our bikes and raised some bunnies. The garage was also used to store my brother's muscle car, and eventually the Ford Gran Torino my dad purchased as Steve and Cathy approached driving age, 'inherited' by me after they broke it in. Next to the garage was a grassy area filled with old scrap metal and farm equipment awaiting its season. Equipment like a field rake or disc harrow, hay wagons, and a manure spreader. There were often high weeds, most of them stinging nettles, in between the equipment. We'd weave our way to the clubhouse, following each other to the secret space. We had to elude the protective red-winged blackbirds who had babies in a nest or a swarm of bees that hid in the scrap metal. My little brother, Alan, believed that holding his breath while taking the path was a sure way to avoid these hazards, especially the sharp itching from the stinging nettles. I suspect it was because he was tinier and following one of us who had already cleared the path! Behind all these obstacles, the clubhouse was out of sight for the most part. Out of eye sight and 'outta sight!' It was worth the effort to get to this concealed shack. We often spent hours here in our own world. We'd prepare pretend meals and serve them on old cracked plates and cups or rusted items we had found around the farm. Old cigar boxes held treasures we found in the pasture or junk piles. The clubhouse had a small loft maybe four feet off the ground, where the chickens once laid their eggs. We could climb up there and rest, often reading comic books and *The Hardy Boys* or *Nancy Drew* mysteries. The old coop was a play haven. We appreciated the privacy and ability to skirt a few chores if no one could find us.

Life Lesson: Create your own 'outta sight' space.

Make time for YOU.

Other times, you could find us riding our bikes down the patchwork of cement sidewalk in the front yard, riding in circles around the green grass or through an obstacle course we had set up with toys and the picnic table. Sometimes we added a home-made jump or two. We maneuvered the course with training wheels until we learned to master that two-wheeled thing. We could get going pretty fast. The novelty of pedaling backwards to put on the brakes wore off and I discovered that dragging the toes of my shoes added an extra dimension to both the timing of avoiding an obstacle and getting a new pair of shoes. I'm sure my mother did not appreciate that discovery!

The large pine in the front yard, which had saved my dad and his siblings from a tornado years before, held a tire swing on one side and was home plate of our baseball field on the other. Here we would run the 'bases' made of various sizes and types of trees. We usually only had a team of two against one batter, so it was exciting when cousins or farm friends stopped by to join us. Just on the outskirts of the baselines sat our swing set on one side and our old two-sided bench swing on the other. The swing set brought hours of entertainment as we swung into the air and launched ourselves forward when high in the sky. Our goal was to jump high enough and far enough to cross the small sidewalk in front of the swing set. For a few years, my siblings tried to jump a small pine that was there.

There were stories of conquering this feat, but never witnesses. Our own fish tale, of sorts.

L-R Sharon, Joyce, Linda, and Terry

Life Lesson: Be carefree! Free from worries, free from anxiety. Carefree is the best kind of FREE.

For the adults, summer competition was based on the timing of planting the fields—which farmer would get their seeds tucked into the ground before a spring storm, but had waited long enough to ensure a spring freeze did not rob them of the fruits of their labor. A common saying for corn farmers in the Midwest is "knee-high by the Fourth of July." It serves as a measurement to determine the quality of the crop compared to previous years. On Sundays, after church, my dad took us on drives to evaluate the health of the neighboring farmers' fields. Cousins, friends, and neighbors came to take pictures of the cornstalks' progress to determine who had earned bragging rights each year.

Ken (front left) and the neighoring farmers

There were other magical places on the farm where we enjoyed our freedom—the woodshed, the two-seater outhouse (when not in use by my father!), the storage shed, and the old unused stone milk house, which lay on the knoll at the end of our front yard. Inevitably, though, there would be a call to the picnic table. My mom carried bucket after bucket of green beans, peas, or sweet corn from the garden. We would snap, snap, snap or shuck, shuck, shuck for what seemed like hours. I have terrific memories of my

Grandma Zander guiding us in the best way to snap a bean. She was quick and steady with her years of experience. She made the garden job tolerable, keeping us occupied at the table and allowing us to help her carry the bowls of fresh beans or peas into the kitchen for freezer and canning preparation.

The long days of summer also meant more hours of farm work. When not in the barn, my father and older siblings were out in the fields, fixing a fence, picking up rocks, baling or stacking hay, and a variety of other opportunities in nice weather. My dad would return to the field after evening milking to plow, or disc, or plant into the early morning. I'm not even sure he slept some nights in order to take advantage of a cool summer evening versus the heat of the day, or maybe to get ahead of a storm rolling in. No Doze pills helped him stay awake and alert, but they were a temporary fix. My dad was good at taking advantage of opportunities to rest and you might find him sleeping in five-minute increments. On rainy days after lunch, a favorite plaid cushioned rocking chair provided the perfect place to relax and rest his weary legs on the ottoman in front of him.

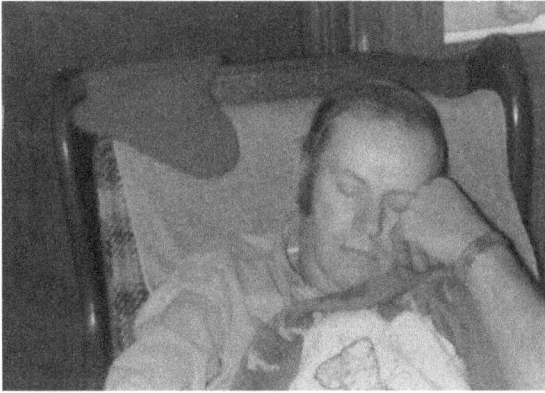

More often, he was found at the kitchen table, up-right with chin to chest, holding the newspaper in his left hand and propping up the right side of the paper with his hook, fast asleep!

Life Lesson: When you work hard, you can rest easy.

Before I was capable to help with the vast array of summer farm work, my job was to deliver the Thermos, a very used and dusty insulated jug, full of ice-cold water to the field. At times, the water was replaced with fresh-squeezed lemonade made with love from the farm kitchen. This was my dad's favorite summer refreshment. It was a staple item at our family picnics. Here's the recipe:

Zander Lemonade

- Squeeze the juice of 3-4 lemons into a 2-quart pitcher.

- Add the juice of 1 navel orange. Remove all seeds!

- Measure ¾-1 cup of granulated sugar and with 2 cups of water to dissolve.

- Add sugar mixture to the pitcher, fill to the top with plenty of ice and water.

- Cut one of the squeezed lemons into quarters and add for extra flavor.

- Pour and serve. Delicious!

From our kitchen window, we could see the hill that called us to explore its features. At the crest of the hill, a large indentation that we referred to as the "Indian Fort" provided ample opportunity to let our imaginations run wild with the endless possibilities of how the cowboys and indians had conquered this hill. The hillside and fort were filled with summer prairie flowers, grasses and large rocks too big to budge, no matter how hard we tried. Here, we would hunker down for cover from the cowboys who were sure to arrive soon. The split rock at the very top made for a great telescope to ensure we could jump out in surprise using long sticks as bows and arrows. We envisioned the rocks were once used by Indians

as natural appliances. A flat, smoother one for cooking in the hot summer sun. Another with three large
dips in it was surely the place the indians had stone
scrubbed their clothing. We would gather up fist-
sized sandstone rocks and grind them in these holes
until they became small grains. Who could grind the
fastest and build the largest pile of sand? From the
fort, we could see my dad working in the fields and my
mom hanging freshly laundered clothes on the four
clothes lines strung between two T-shaped metal
poles 20 feet apart. Peace in the valley. The sublime
beauty of the rolling hills and patchwork of crops in
the fields could be seen for miles and miles.

Life Lesson: Nature is magical.

By age eight, I had joined in on the rotation
of around-the-clock chores. Not by demand, but by
choice. Farm life was all I knew, and I wanted to be
a part of it, at least at first. I started with the simple
jobs of replacing a bucket of udder-washing water or
retrieving a certain tool needed for a mechanical repair. The chores evolved into the more physical tasks
of scraping the cow manure out of the alleys into the
trough-like gutter, carrying barrels of sileage into the
feed alley on the front side of the cow stanchions, and
lifting bale after bale of hay on hay-making days.

Hay days—a series of prime summer days when the
fields were dry and the hay knee-high. My father or
one of my brothers would hook up the chopper behind the red International Harvester tractor. Driving
in a straight line down a field, the chopper would

slice the alfalfa at the base and spit it into neat rows about five feet wide. Then, the sun did its job to dry it out. A day later, another machine, the rake, was pulled by its tractor beside these neat rows. It narrowed the rows and flipped the hay over, allowing the sunrays to beat down on this side for a day. Weather permitting, the third day was baling day. Behind the baler, already hooked up to the tractor with the hitch and pin, a third piece of equipment, the hay wagon, was attached. This was the third time through the same field; the baler was now able to do its job of collecting the tangled alfalfa into chunks and tying twine around approximately 10 chunks into a bale. The bales were ejected from the baler chute and flew through the air until hitting the tall back of the hay wagon where it would drop down to the base or on top of other bales that had already found their destination.

There were times the weather didn't cooperate. Rain on already chopped hay required extra days for drying and the rake would return for another visit to the field, tossing it over, yet again, from the underside. Until now, I never realized how important the timing was or the complexity of the process for harvesting alfalfa. I just knew how it felt to see wagon after wagon being pulled into the farm driveway awaiting the next part of the process—getting the hay into its winter storage place, the hayloft. Around the backside of the barn, someone had already backed the hay elevator up to the barn window on the high end of the barn. The long conveyor belt had a mechanized chain with dull three-inch spikes spaced to grab each bale and take it for a ride to the hay-loft. How did the bales make it to the conveyor, you ask? The muscles and sweat of this farmgirl, of course! The first bales fell off the wagon easily, and if the wagon was positioned properly, they plopped onto the elevator and up they would go. The other 50 bales or so on each wagon had to be hand-tossed onto that elevator. Bale after bale, load after wagon load, I would grab the two twines around the bale, carry each to the edge of the wagon, and swing it onto one of those rotating spikes. Up in the hayloft, the bales dropped into a pile and were then carried to their resting place by a sibling or hired hand, neatly stacked to the ceiling of the second story of the barn. Growing up, most of my siblings and I did not want to be associated with farming or the constant physical labor that came with it. Today, we all share the loyal work ethic with the businesses and professions we chose. There ain't no desk job that is harder than forking shit or baling hay.

I quickly learned that while I was sweating it out under the hot summer sun, my classmates were riding bikes, at the pool, or taking family vacations across the country. I was lucky if I could take a few hours on a summer afternoon to ride my bike into town and hang out with them. Bike-riding amnesty! Not an official pardon, but when out bike riding, there was no way for anyone to know where I was. My battery-operated AM/FM bike radio attached to the handlebars with the long wire antenna swinging in the tire-induced breeze, intermittently picking up the air waves providing the music.

Our family vacations were few and far between. They mostly involved a day trip in-between morning and evening milking sessions. Seven hours to get to a destination, 'vacation,' and drive back. Picnics at Governor Dodge State Park or Brigham County Park were favorites. Some summers we ventured a bit farther to the Milwaukee County Zoo or our Keating cousins' cabin on Lake Holcomb. Other times, my mom was able to load three or four of us into the panel-sided station wagon, with a tractor innertube tied to the top with hay twine, and take us to swim and relax at nearby Fish Lake.

There were a lot of opportunities for competition on the farm—racing to the barn, stacking hay bales, and washing a cow udder faster than the others. Our favorite competition came on summer nights after the evening milking. A before-dark game of family badminton in the backyard with Dad. Taking turns batting the "birdie" across the net and stretching to reach the out-of-control target. Winning team scored 21 points. At dusk, my siblings and I repeatedly played a game we called Oly Oly Ocean Free (similar to Kick the Can). While writing this book, I investigated the history of this game and found this excerpt on the internet. (Dave Tabler, "Ollie Ollie Come in Free!" Appalachian History. June 21, 2017, http://www.appalachianhistory.net/2017/06/ollie-ollie-in-come-free.html)

*When I was growing up in the American South,"
says Charles Wilson in The New Encyclopedia of
Southern Culture, "we actually said, 'All ye all
ye outs in free' when playing hide-and-seek (although we called it 'hide-and-go-seek)." Regional
variations include:*

- Ollie Ollie in come free,
- Ollie Ollie oxenfreed,
- Ollie ollie in come free-o
- Ollie ollie oxen free
- Ollie ollie oxen free-o
- Oly Oly oxen free,
- Oly Oly ocean free,
- Alley Alley oats in free,
- All-ye All-ye outs in free
- Ole Ole Olsen free (more common in areas settled by Scandinavians)
- Ole Ole Olsen free-o

*Children's sayings were hardly recorded until
the 1950s, and they are very variable. That's because they've been passed down orally from one
generation to the next, with no adult interven-
tion or correction. But one educated guess is that
the phrase's root is an English-Norman French-
Dutch/German concoction: "Alles, Alles, in
kommen frei" or "Alle, alle auch sind frei" (literally, "Everyone, everyone also is free") or
"Oyez, oyez, in kommen frei!"*

Our version of Oly Oly Ocean Free looked like this:

One person is 'it' and tried to find the others, who had spread out and hidden in the darkest spots we could find. Under a clump of the largest rhubarb patch in the valley or behind the bicycles neatly nested beneath the enclosed basement staircase. Up on the porch roof or under the large piece of sheet metal that covered the basement window well. Only the bravest ventured into the darkness of the barn or machine shed. Once hidden, we awaited the perfect opportunity to sneak into 'goal' before the seeker touched us.

Life Lesson: A family that plays together, stays together.

Inside the farmhouse, my bedroom was muggy and stale on summer evenings. If we were lucky, the wind blowing from the east or south created the luxury of a cross breeze. My sister, Cathy, and I shared a small bedroom with one small double-hung window. We propped up the old framework of the window with a box fan in hopes of drawing in the summer air. Placed at the foot of our bed, we often moved our pillows to the other end to feel the breeze on our faces, settling into a peaceful sleep while we listened to crickets and frogs chatter. We slept well from the fresh air, constant activity, and freedom from worry. We had everything we needed.

Life Lesson: Appreciate the simple things in life.

◆ ◆ ◆

Do-A-Dab

dab: *noun*

> 1. a small amount of something.
> *"She licked a dab of chocolate from her finger."*
> —Google Dictionary

There is a lot to dabble in on a farm, from cows to combines, from hogs to hay. Discs to dung. Silage to stones. Field work to farmyard. Barns to beef. Start working on any one of them and soon you'll uncover another. The abundance of small tasks, when combined, turn into a full day of chores to keep a small family business running. So much to do. So little time. I'm sure I don't even know the half of it. I never saw the farm as a business until I had moved away. My mom and dad took care of a lot behind the scenes. My mom, being the chief financial officer of the farm, maintained a meticulous record of every expense and source of income, no matter how small. My dad made the decisions on every purchase and managed the physical labor, including the tasks of his eight children. Terry, Linda, and Joyce certainly experienced more manual labor than me. Sharon, Steve, and Cathy had some reprieve as our clan grew and the chores spread amongst them. Each of us were paid a 'salary' to work on the farm. We received $30/month—of which $15 each month had to be deposited into Anchor Savings and Loan. In this way, they were teaching us that they valued our contributions, and at the same time, teaching us to save. The other $15 was paid in cash, and we each had an envelope that mom kept in the cupboard by the dishes.

By the time I was old enough to help, the combination of technology and farm improvements had eased even more of the burden. Still, the long days, steady routine, and constant chores are not forgiving. Seven days a week and 14-hour days are the routine. Longer days crept in while planting in the spring and harvesting in the fall. This is not a sympathy trip, it is reality. A farmer chooses this lifestyle and appreciation for the land. S/He is a true conservationist—protecting the soil and its interacting organisms. In turn, this protects many of our ecosystems—water, air, nutrients, plants, rocks, fungi, and animals. A farmer is a scientist in the truest form. A farmer constantly studies the sequence of events to gather data and adjusts their methods to leverage the current conditions of the ecosystem. Eventually, s/he becomes an expert in their field. No pun intended.

Perhaps the best way to describe what a farmer does, and why, is in the *Farmer's Creed* written for Sperry New Holland, an agricultural machinery manufacturer, and originally published in October 1975.

Farmer's Creed

I believe a man's greatest possession is his dignity and that no calling bestows this more abundantly than farming.

I believe hard work and honest sweat are the building blocks of a person's character.

I believe farming, despite its hardships and disappointments, is the most honest and honorable way a man can spend his days on this earth.

I believe farming nurtures the close family ties that make life rich in ways money can't buy.

I believe my children are learning values that will last a lifetime and can be learned in no other way.

I believe farming provides education for life and that no other occupation teaches so much about birth, growth, and maturity in such a variety of ways.

I believe many of the best things in life are indeed free: the splendor of a sunrise, the rapture of wide-open spaces, the exhilarating sight of your land greening each spring.

I believe true happiness comes from watching your crops ripen in the field, your children grow tall in the sun, your whole family feels the pride that springs from their shared experience.

I believe that by my toil I am giving more to the world than I am taking from it, an honor that does not come to all men.

I believe my life will be measured ultimately by what I have done for my fellow man, and by this standard I fear no judgment.

I believe when a man grows old and sums up his day, he should be able to stand tall and feel pride in the life he's lived.

I believe in farming because it makes all this possible.

Permission to reprint granted by CNH Industrial America LLC.

It did—make it possible. My family reaped all those benefits and more. A typical day, if there were one, might look like this:

The night is nearly ended, with the moon still lingering before the sun arises in the east. The brass-rimmed, round alarm clock clicks into position and the double-clap ringer bounces from bell to bell, making an obnoxious racket. My mother hops out of bed and takes two steps to the dresser where she taps the thick, stick-pin-like stem on the top of the alarm clock to stop the ringing. She begins her day by nudging my dad out of bed and assisting him in attaching his hollow prosthetic arm with the metal hook. Before descending the curved farmhouse stairs to the kitchen, my mother knocks on the bedroom door of the sibling who is 'it' for morning chore rotation. She heads downstairs to toast a slice of bread and prepare a glass of milk for my dad, who is already halfway out the door. By now, the sibling who is on morning chores rotation for that day is supposed to be putting their barn coat on. But, almost always, my mom returns to the second-story bedroom to awaken them and remind them of their duty. This is more of a ruckus than it needs to be, and by now, the rest of us are wide awake, too. Anyone over six years of age is up and at 'em by 6:30 a.m.

Life Lesson: Rise and shine—literally!

The large front porch doubled as an office and held two 10-foot-long closets, one on each side of the room. The one on the right held all the smelly farm attire. Shelves full of the manure covered mid-calf boots, otherwise known as shit kickers. Other weather-related clothing needed for the season, such as overcoats, shoe rubbers, and bandanas for the girls' hair, as well as hats for the boys. This pit stop was necessary for preparing for what we'd be up against in the barn. My dad and oldest brother Terry already had the cows in their stanchions and the milk parlor was humming—waiting for the first drops of that precious white gold. We had 62 cow stanchions, and each was occupied with a cow and its full udder, ready for the machines to do the work. Four milk machines had been sanitized the night before and were attached to the stainless steel pail that would capture the milk. The four machines had replaced the hand milking that my father and his siblings had endured in earlier years.

On school mornings, Cathy and I helped get the milking started and then turned to feeding the calves with the fresh milk. The calves were kept in one of four pens, depending on age. These were located on the far end of the barn until 1976, when we removed a small brick silo and built an addition off the side of the barn. Depending on their age, the calves were bottle- or bucket-fed. The bottles were three-four quarts each and filled in the milk parlor with the fresh cow milk, which had been carried to the cooler in the stainless-steel pails. As the calf grew older, a milk replacer, like baby formula, might be used. After filling the bottle, a pliable rubber nipple, approximately three inches long with a base approximately three inches in diameter, was snapped onto the top. Metal hangers attached to the calf stanchions to hold the bottles in place, allowing several calves to 'nurse' at once. The inevitable calf or two that did not take to the bottle had to be coerced. This consisted of ensuring the other calves were secure in their stanchions and eagerly drinking from a small calf pail or a hanging bottle. After entering the calf pen, I cornered a calf and straddled it with my legs. I'd insert two fingers into its mouth to get it suckling and then try to replace my fingers with the three-inch nipple of the bottle. Once the nipple was placed, I'd gently rub the calf's long, soft throat to assist in swallowing its large gulps of milk. One down, sometimes as many as five more to go. Then, I'd quickly dump some calf pellets and ground corn in the feed alley and get back to the house by 6:50. There was often no time for a shower to get ready for the bus by 7:10. Somewhere in there, we may have eaten something. I cannot recall.

Dad was a progressive leader in his profession. He was often the first in our area to buy state-of-the art farm equipment, add new buildings, and try new technologies. In the early '50s, he installed a stainless-steel bulk tank milk cooler. It was larger than most and touted as modern and sanitary. The cooler had a super large rotating paddle which slowly stirred the milk as fresh warm milk was mixed into any previously cooled milk. The milk was stored and refrigerated here for up to three days before the milk truck arrived for pick up.

Charleen holding Joyce, Terry, Linda, and Ken

Raising pigs was another investment my father made. The sale of pork was often higher than beef, so eventually he built a large, new pig shed. This, too, was state-of-the art as the floors on the outer sides of each pigpen slowly slanted down and into a large center gutter that would carry the manure to the outside of the barn. Ten years later, we added a corn mill right next to the new pig barn—grinding our own feed. John O'Donnell, a salesman who worked for Feed-O-Matic, came to visit often and helped Dad install the feed mill. He also shared the news of a legume that was becoming more popular in our area. We became early growers of soybeans as an alternative feed for the cows and hogs. We installed our own soybean roaster. The large, funnel-shaped bin roasted the soybeans into a delicious snack before it was ground into meal for the animals. I remember climbing up the outside of the large grain wagon, called a gravity box, and scooping up a handful of these warm, tasty roasted beans! People pay good money for a bag of this healthy treat in stores now.

Life Lesson: Take educated risks—be innovative to grow your business.

Up to now, "on-farm roasting" of livestock feed has been limited primarily to soybeans—at least in Wisconsin.

But now Kenneth Zander, first state farmer to install a soybean roaster, also likes results he's gotten from roasting shelled corn for certain parts of his hog, dairy, and beef operations.

We described Zander's experience with roasting soybeans shortly after he put a new gas-fired soybean roaster into operation in 1969. Here's an updated report on how roasting soybeans and shelled corn are working out for him.

The roaster, along with an electric feed mill, gives Zander a complete on-farm feed processing system. He buys only limited protein for his dairy herd.

Roasts soybeans for all livestock

Zander roasts whole soybeans that go into ration of 300 feeder pigs being finished for market, 40 milk cow herd, young stock, and 60 head of beef being fed out.

"There's no real savings for buying raw soybeans at present prices instead of soybean meal," says Zander. "But it's the improvement in performance of livestock and lower feed costs by processing my own feed that make roasting soybeans pay."

For example, Zander points to faster daily gains and improved feed efficiency of his feeder pigs.

"All pigs I sent to market last year on roasted soybeans averaged about 1.8 pounds of gain a day," says Zander. "This compares with 1.5 to 1.6 pounds per day gain for feeder pigs I sent to market before I had the roaster."

Zander has continued to buy the same type of feeder pigs from the same farmers. He feeds out groups of 50 hogs in 6 different pens (300 total pigs) in a confined feeding operation.

Keeping good records has also let Zander pinpoint a savings of about $2 per hog in improved feed efficiency. It takes that much less feed since I've used roasted soybeans to get a hog to market weight of 200 to 225 pounds, he says.

Zander starts 40-pound feeders out on a 16% protein ration. He shifts them to a 15% protein diet at 100 pounds, a 14% ration at 130 pounds, and 12% to 13% ration at 180 pounds.

Healthier pigs may be another benefit realized from feeding roasted soybeans. Zander can't explain the reason for this. A vantage from including roasted soybeans in the ration of his dairy herd.

"Cows have higher butterfat test when on roasted soybeans," he explains. "Fat test of my herd held at 3.8 to 3.9% all of 1970 when they were on roasted soybeans." Zander switched the dairy herd to commercial supplement last January to see what influence roasted beans had. "Test dropped to 3.5 to 3.6% since I took the cows off roasted beans."

Zander hasn't noticed any difference in total milk production since he took cows off roasted beans in January. He plans to put the dairy herd back on roasted beans next lactation.

Beef cattle and young stock also get roasted beans. Zander doesn't keep records on these phases so he isn't certain if there's an advantage.

Roasts corn for calves, young pigs

Success with roasting soybeans prompted Zander to roast corn. "Since I feed considerable shelled corn, I roast it only for young pigs, calves, and beef cattle."

Since he started in January, Zander has found advantages for roasting corn for calves and young pigs. "I've been able to make my own calf starter ration at a considerable savings over purchased starters by using roast-

$6 for a hundred pounds of commercial calf starter.

A 2025-pound batch of his starter ration consists of 1100 pounds of roasted and cracked shelled corn, 475 pounds of oats (he'd like to use more oats but he's short of it), 400 pounds of roasted whole soybeans, and 50 pounds of minerals.

Calves went on this starter ration in January. "Calves like it. They're well filled out and have a slick hair coat," says Zander. He's not certain, however, if calves gain any better on it than commercial starters.

But Zander has noticed that young pigs gain faster on roasted corn. "I get feeders from 40 to 80 pounds in about 5 less days since I've been feeding roasted corn," he says.

Pigs put on the 40 pounds in about 20 days now compared to about 25 days when they got regular corn. Zander believes that roasting changes starch in corn to a more usable form of sugar.

Zander put the first group of feeder pigs on roasted corn in February. He's noticed the same increased gains in several other batches he purchased since.

When pigs reach 80 pounds, they're taken off the roasted corn diet. By that time they're able to utilize regular corn nearly as well as roasted corn, says Zander.

Beef cattle have been on roasted corn ration for about 2 months.

Roasted soybeans are augered directly to a holding bin above this electric feed mill. There they are ground and blended into desired ration for swine, dairy and beef cattle by Dane county farmer Kenneth Zander.

John and the entire O'Donnell family became our friends. He and his wife, Betty, lived in the city of Madison with their kids. We would take turns making family visits. Sharon, Steve, Cathy, and I got to stay overnight at their home and enjoy the park and pool right down their street. I took my first city bus ride with Mary Pat O'Donnell to a local convenience store to purchase some candy called Fizzies Drink Tablets. These were made to add to water and create a drink like soda pop, but we just nibbled off bits of the tart round disc and let it fizz in our mouth. Delicious!

The O'Donnell kids also would visit the farm and stay overnight with us. They were curious about the milking operation and would join their dad on his frequent business visits. On one such occasion, John was discussing the variety of chores required on a farm. He said to my dad, "Well, I guess you have a lot of kids to help get them done. If they each do a little here, or do a dab there, they can get a whole lot done. Here a dab, there a dab—Do-a-dab!" Do-A-Dab Farm was born. Terry was in high school and decided to craft a large farm sign in shop class. He erected the sign to hang from chain links attached to a wooden frame which hung in the corner of our driveway. "Do-A-Dab Farm – Kenneth F. Zander Family" was painted in black across the large white background of the six-foot-wide-by-six-foot-tall wooden identifier.

On weekends, we stuck around to help with all the other daily chores that my mom and dad took care of on schooldays. The entire milking process took approximately two hours, and, upon finishing, the cows were released to the cow yard to eat a trough full of sileage—the ground corn we had saved from the harvest the previous year. Some days, the bull was also released from the far end of the barn to breed with the cows. We had several bulls over the years, but the one we all remember was intense and wild. I would hide in the milk house as several of my siblings grabbed pitchforks to guide the bull into the cow yard or back to his pen when he finished.

The cows had two different pastures. The one across the road and up the hillside (which you'll learn more about in the next chapter) and another down a lane to the creek. Creekside provided fresh water throughout the day along with the prairie grasses running along what is now called the Black Earth Trout Creek. The cows had fresh grass in either pasture and we rotated between the two to ensure consistent growth for future grazing opportunities.

Once the barn was empty, we could clean and prepare for the next milking, which would begin in approximately 10 hours. The long-handled scraper with a blade three feet wide was used to move manure from the main aisle between the cow stanchions, as well as the cow stanchions themselves, into the gutter. The gutter was a trough made between two sides of 18-inch-deep concrete, strategically placed behind the cows' back legs while they were standing with their heads locked in their stanchion. The gutter was equipped with a series of paddles chain-linked together that moved manure and other waste toward a chute at the end of the barn that emptied into a manure spreader. As the manure was moved to the outside, work on the inside continued. A coat of white barn lime was spread across the main aisles and stanchions to dry out the concrete and make for a clean environment for the next milking. The lime provided a fresh layer to absorb the scents and excretions of the cows. In the winter, bedding of cornstalks was placed in each stanchion to provide warmth for the cows. The bedding was carried by large pitch forks from the bedding room to each of the 62 stanchions. I remember timing myself while doing this chore to see if I could beat my previous record. Probably not the safest thing to do with a pitchfork in hand!

Our barn was kept super clean! There were health standards to meet. When the USDA farm inspector arrived, s/he was impressed with my dad's standard for cleanliness and sanitation. We made it easy for the inspector to provide high ratings and rarely had a 'red mark' on the inspection report. We scraped and swept and sanitized more than required. My dad left nothing to chance—the sanitization routine was crucial to our farm's success. The milk carrier tested our milk every day to make sure there was no contamination. A small test tube with some litmus paper verified its quality on the spot.

Life Lesson: If you are going to do a job, do the job well. No halfsies.

After morning milking was completed on weekends, usually between 9-10 a.m., it was time for breakfast of fresh eggs and toast. We usually ate in shifts, depending on which job we were assigned.

On Saturdays, Linda, Joyce, Sharon, Cathy, and I were assigned household chores of cleaning and laundry. Somehow, Mom already had laundry off to a good start by the time we dug in. We helped iron select laundered items, from hankies to church dress clothes, folded and sorted laundry into piles of clean clothing, and stacked the clothes on the dining room table, providing a personalized stack for each of us to carry to our rooms later. We put clean sheets on the beds and baked cookies. We were each assigned a section of the house to clean—upstairs, downstairs, Grandma's Side, the porches, or the bathrooms. In my teenage years, after Grandma Zander passed away, one of us would be assigned to hop on our bicycle and pedal up the road to clean Grandma Brunner's house, too.

Terry and Steve had their own outdoor assignments. They included driving the manure spreader out to the fields to spread the sloppy, smelly stuff across the soil for fertilizer or shoveling out the manure from the calf barn across the road. There were no gutters in this calf shed—the shit literally got flung

out of the window by hand! Scraping and hosing out
the pig barn was another sloppy job. Even Alan, the
spoiled one, joined them when he was old enough to
lift and push the heavy piles. These things were required daily or, at a minimum, every other day to
keep up with the animal's defecation.

Depending on summer or winter, there were a variety of other chores. Baling and stacking hay, load-
ing a silo, fixing a tractor, planting a field, cultivating, raking, picking rocks out of a field, or the tall
yellow plant we referred to as mustard seed out of the
crops, harvesting, mowing the lawn, pulling weeds
along the wired fence line, gardening, pushing snow,
cleaning out a shed, tagging cattle, and testing milk.
The list was endless and regimented and sometimes
interrupted if a repair was needed. Dad allowed us to
take breaks from chores throughout the weekend. We
might read a book in the hay mound, play make-believe spy, build hay forts, or spend some time swinging from the posts in the barn or doing summersaults
around the cow stanchions. There were a lot of ways
to entertain ourselves.

Zander Farm - circa 1978

At about 4 in the afternoon, it was back to the barn. In the silo room, we'd load up bushel barrels full of silage to deliver to each cow's feeding stanchion. On top of each pile of silage went a scoop of minerals, fresh ground corn, or both. Up in the hay mound, we'd carry bales of hay to the chute, cut open the twine, and release slices of compressed alfalfa down into the feed alleys. There were four hay chutes, one for every 14 cows. We also threw bales down the hay loft stairs to reach the side feed alley for the remaining six cows. The hay then had to be spread and shaken out by pitchfork along the feed alley so that it was within reach of each heifer. While this was going on, one of us had been sent to gather and follow the cows home from the pasture.

Evening milking would begin as soon as we finished eating one of Mom's homecooked meals around the dinner table. After another two-hour milking session, the cows were released back to the enclosed pasture on summer nights or, in the winter, remained head-locked in their stanchions in the barn. The herd created its own warmth to keep from freezing.

After milking, our family gathered in the living room where some watched TV, some did homework, and some of us (ME!) sat on Dad's lap to share a bowl of popcorn. I'm sure my dad was exhausted, but he was proud of the day's accomplishments and loved this evening family time together.

Life Lesson: Take pride in your day's work.

Bringing the Cows Home

"*C*ome bosss, *come* boooosss." That was the rally cry I'd shout across the hillside as I tried to locate the large group of Holsteins that managed their way to the far back corner of our property. What was better about that grass back there? I don't know, but they always seemed to venture as far as the fences allowed them. One of my favorite memories of growing up on Zander Do-A-Dab Farm is bringing the cows home. It was an opportunity to escape the rest of the chores on the farm—to experience a bit of peace and freedom. Don't get me wrong, amongst my siblings and I, this was still considered a chore, yet one of the better ones if we had a choice. Unless, of course, it was raining or stormy. If one was lucky, it involved a ride to the other end of our property by tractor, if fieldwork was occurring in the area. Or by car, if Mom was not busy gardening, cooking, or doing laundry. Other times, we walked the mile or so to find the cows in the far back field. Usually, you could see the black and white spots somewhere in the woods for an indication of their whereabouts. Every once in a while, they appeared "lost" and it meant there would be several attempts of getting them to respond to me shouting, "*Come*, booooss, *come*, booooosssss" and then, "*heerrre*, bossie, bossie, bossie."

(Merriam-Webster lists cow as one of the definitions for the English noun "boss," citing the first know use as 1790. "Coboss," a shortened version of the two words "come, boss" meaning "a call to cows" appears in the dictionary as well. *Boss* came from the word for cow in Latin, *bos*, a term that can also mean ox and bull. Cattle are part of the genus *Bos*, and are usually classified as *Box Taurus*.)

Sometimes, my calling them became much more intense, almost angry, but eventually it would lead to a moo or two in return. Where there is one moo there is another, and they always gave their location away. The well-rehearsed line children learn from Old McDonald's Farm nursery rhyme is a real thing—*Here a moo, there a moo, everywhere a moo moo.*

Once you knew where they were, it was a matter of 'kicking them up'—not literally, of course. Getting them to move sometimes involved a slap on the backside of one so she'd take off and rile the rest of the herd to get moving. The cows knew the way home and I simply followed them home through the woods and over the hills.

At times, a Holstein would take sanctuary in the thicket of woods, where they had given birth to a calf or were found ill. They were left behind until the newborn calf had stable legs to follow its mother home, or until the cattle truck we used to take the beef cattle to market could come back to retrieve them.

I loved meandering across the hills and pastures, following the herd home. It was my time to dream and lollygag. I would belt out songs and carry on a conversation with nature. Thankfully, it was only me and the cows who could hear my random thoughts and lack of musical tunes as I'd weave through the patch of woods.

Life Lesson: Sing as if no one is listening.

Trails had been beaten and cleared by the hooves that repeatedly tromped this ground and passed this way thousands of times. The trails were rocky, muddy, slanted, and uphill both ways, I swear! Some were more difficult to navigate then others due to downed branches and plenty of old and new 'cow pies.' One could not daydream for too long or you could easily take a misstep into the still-steaming, pie-shaped plops of manure. Thank goodness for those shitkickers, which doubled as hiking boots.

The scenery along the trails varied depending on the time of year. The budding new leaves and bright green grasses of spring still allowed a view of a rolling hill, a field, or even a car or two on the local road. The thickness of full growth and random undergrowth in the late summer, where one could find a great hiding place and oftentimes our birthing cows bedded down here. My favorite time of year was the fall, with the leaves changing colors and falling to cover the trail in the colors of the season. There were hickory nuts to pocket or acorns that made a great little miniature pipe when carved out with a hickory nut picker and with a matchstick inserted as the mouthpiece. In the winter, the cows stayed in the barn or close to home, as reserved silage was their primary form of nutrition. No matter what time of the year, my favorite spot along the way was when I'd round the corner after leaving the lane at the 'other place,' the second farm my grandfather had purchased and added to our acreage in the 1950s. Here, there were shooting stars and honeysuckle on the hillside that stretched toward the sun. In late afternoon the sun, was cresting the hill and this place made for a shady rest stop. A quiet moment to overlook the valley and take a break.

Life Lesson: Pick a flower. Enjoy the view.

If I didn't sit too long, I could walk to the top of the hill, which had the best view of the farmhouse, barns, and outbuildings. This view of the valley took my breath away. It warmed my soul, just like that feeling you get when you eat your favorite comfort food. There were times in my life when I did not appreciate this land or the view. As a typical teenager, I had friends I wanted to see, school events I wished I could attend, or a boyfriend on my mind. Yet, I was oh-so-blessed with this beautiful land, home, and family. It was also from this viewpoint that I could see the cows had all made it down the hill, through the third cow lane of this journey and into the cow yard across from the farmhouse. I was supposed to be there too and so I'd run down the hill in hopes of no one having seen me lollygag. At the end of the lane, I'd secure the wooden gate so the cows remained fenced in near the barn and close by the fresh water in the eight-foot-long cement cow tank attached to the side of the calf barn. In the summer, this small, flat pasture was more than a cow corral. It was a passersby landmark, calling people to its boundaries, as well. Over the years, artists stopped along the barbed wire fence to paint portraits of the countryside. Married couples with a baby on the way stopped to watch a cow give birth. These couples would stand for hours, not only watching the birth, but the calf being licked clean by its mother and then its wobbly ascent to stand, finding its mother's udder and beginning to suckle. I didn't realize then how the land and nature could call a person to it. It was all I knew, and so didn't everyone? To me, it was odd that people found this entertaining or interesting or both.

Life Lesson: Our life experiences—our stories—are unique and worthy of sharing.

Near the water tank, which was attached to the calf barn for convenient plumbing to replenish it, I'd

climb over the fence and cross the road to the farmhouse. Supper was usually waiting, but we had one
more chore to do before we would all sit together at
the table. It was cow crossing time.

Our farm was split by County Road KP. It was a
busy road then, before they built Highway 14 just
¼ mile north. Now, it's less traveled. Safety for the
cow crossing was vital. Cows are no track stars. The
crossing was approximately 100 yards on the road,
extending from the pasture on the east side of the
house to the cowyard on the west end of the barn. The
stretch of road the length of a football field could be
seen quite clearly when driving west. However, cars
traveling east would round a sharp corner and have
less than 80 feet to stop before hitting a cow. My siblings would join me from various locations around
the farm, as we needed three to five herders to make
sure the cows moved quickly and safely. One to open
the gate and get behind the herd, one on the east end
so they didn't venture the wrong way towards Cross
Plains, one along the farmhouse yard to make sure the
lawn was off-limits, and one or two at the west end to
guide them into the barn cowyard and secure the gate
behind them. The whole process took about seven to
10 minutes. It was a production and locals were used
to the time of day it occurred. Most of them were
cautious, yet several near misses took place over
the years. Eventually, my dad extended the pasture
around the calf barn and 70 yards further towards the
barn so that the cow crossing was a direct path from

one side of the road to the other. Still a three-minute production, but safer for all of us.

While the cows awaited the opportunity to empty their full udders, our family ate dinner at 5:30 sharp. All my seven siblings, Mom, Dad, Grandma Zander, and I crowded around the undersized table for eight. I had just enough room to squeeze around to the center of the longer back side of the oval oak table to get to my spot. Here, with my back against the one small double-hung kitchen window, I waited until my mom led us in reciting the before meals, and then my she began passing the serving bowls of steaming food. The table was set and a pitcher of fresh, pasteurized milk on it, along with real butter—never anything but the real thing. Steaks from our own beef cattle and vegetables from our own garden were common meals. It's no wonder we didn't like the goulash or fried liver that were served less frequently as substitutes for the quality beef! I'm not sure any of us realized how blessed we were to have fresh, homegrown food on the table every day. This was the one meal we all ate together and it began in prayer, thankful for our table of homegrown farm produce and, looking back, thankful for my mother who prepared it. She seemed to do so effortlessly, and the meal was always dished, served, and passed. Although, I don't recall my mom sitting down to eat. Did she? One thing is for sure—you came quickly to the table when the meal was ready, AND you took your share from the bowl on the first pass or not at all.

Life Lesson: Get it while it's hot!

After dinner, it was back to the barn for the evening milking. Another venture full of life lessons in and of itself.

◆ ◆ ◆

ACRE 7

White Gold

A dairy farmer's bread and butter, literally, is milk. Every drop is precious white gold. Careful timing of milking and grazing, along with rations for feeding, ensure the cows achieve top production. Where they graze, what water source they drink from, the quality of corn and other nutrients they are fed, and the bull they breed with all impact a cow's overall health and quality of milk. High butterfat content makes for better milk quality and a higher selling price.

Life Lesson: Quality work produces quality results.

The act of milking a cow is quite complex. There are a lot of things to take into consideration. Cows have different personalities and temperaments, just like people. Entering a stanchion to wash the udder meant understanding the mood of each cow. Most of the time, they knew it meant relief of their bulging udder and enjoyed the light massage while being washed with the warm antibacterial water. Other cows were crabby, hoisting their obnoxiously large bodies against you or kicking at their space. These cows were a two-person job, with one of us grabbing their tail, curling it up over their backside, and pressing it towards their hips to make it more difficult for them to move.

I used a standard approach and stance while washing a cow's udder by leaning into the cow's left hip with my right hip, placing my right arm up across their back, and patting lightly to comfort them. Then I'd lean down with the left hand and stretch under the udder with a soaked paper towel, rubbing the dirt and crusty manure onto the towel. Several towels might be used on one udder. I repeated this process until the entire surface and each nipple were clean, to ensure quality milk. I stepped out and my dad, Terry, or Steve stepped in to place one of four oblong suction cups on each nipple. The electric motor from the milking system created enough suction to grab hold of each teat and began a series of pulsations to empty the milk through the rubber hose, collecting it into a ten-gallon stainless steel milk pail. After the udder was empty, made obvious by the now-loose and rippled skin of the deflated udder, Cathy, Alan or I dipped each nipple, one at a time, using a dipping cup full of iodine. The iodine protected the teats from bacteria that might seep in and cause mastitis, an infection that meant weeks' worth of lost milk. After 2-3 cows were milked, the stainless-steel milk pail would be swapped for another.

Life Lesson: No matter what job you do, do it well.

When I wasn't washing an udder, I was carrying

the milk. Five to seven gallons at a time. I'd grab the thin, handle of the stainless steel milk pail and swing it from side to side to help build momentum and balance the weight as I walked down the lime-covered aisle to the Step-Saver, a stainless steel cart with a covered tub that was rolled down the center barn aisle and had about 150 feet of milk hose coiled around it. Stepping on a pedal to lift the dust cover on the tub, I'd pour the milk into a large funnel. The milk was sucked out of the bottom of this stainless steel tub and traveled through the 150-foot hose, attached by hooks to the barn beams at above-head height. It was vacuumed all the way to a large glass jar called the milk receiver, then through the sanitary tank, and pumped into the 2,500-gallon cooler in the milk house. When the milk had drained out of the Step-Saver, a big floating ball sealed the funnel to maintain the vacuum pressure of the system. As milking progressed, the cart was pushed down the aisles and more hose extended or retracted, based on the section of the barn where the milking was occurring.

I find it ironic that now I work hard to get 10,000 steps in in a day (as recommended for good health) and the Step-Saver was meant to reduce steps. It did save time, yet I'm pretty sure that had I tracked my steps in the '70s and '80s, my daily average would have exceeded triple what I do today. Steps were reduced even further when our 'pipeline' was installed in 1978. By then, my older siblings had all moved on. Only Alan and I reaped the benefits of this dream of dreams for any farmhand. With this system, the machine on the cow's udder was connected to a rubber hose that we attached directly to the vacuum-packed stainless steel pipe that ran the full 80-foot length of the barn. Approximately every 8 feet, a sealed access port, called a cock stall, provided the suction to attach the transportable hose assembly from the machine to the pipeline. Our barn had two main aisles. The stainless steel pipes extended across the 60-foot width of the barn, as well as the length of the barn and hung above the stanchions for cleanliness and easy access to the cock stall No more carrying milk. It made life easier for daily milking, but with all technology comes new challenges. The pipeline system might spring a leak or capture bacteria, and had its own regime to keep it functioning properly.

Whether a pipeline, Step-Saver, or a full walk to the stainless steel milk tank was used, all milk handling systems were cleaned and sanitized after every milking session. This was my job on weekend mornings and most week nights. In the milkhouse, I would place the end of the hose that was used to transfer the milk into a cleaning system. Water would pump through the now-curled-up hose, or through the stainless steel pipes, to push sanitary solutions through. I also attached each udder cup on each of the six milking machines to a stainless-steel flushing system. The washing system first rinsed out the remaining milk and then flushed cleaning solution through the piping to kill bacteria and remove milkstone, a layer of scale mainly formed by calcium and magnesium in the milk. The entire washing mechanism was operated very much like a household dishwasher on a much larger scale.

The barreled semi backed into our driveway at approximately 11 a.m. every day. The hauler jumped down from the cab with a test bag ready to collect a sample from our large refrigerated tank. The milk house had been hosed down and sanitized before he arrived and inside the door hung a clip board with the daily gallon count and time collected. A small sample was collected by the hauler with a stainless steel ladle and poured in the three-by-five-inch bag. The hauler grabbed the two tabs at the top of the bag and swirled it over several times to seal it. The bag was labeled "Ken Zander Farm" and placed in a small cooler bin on the side of the truck. Next, the hauler unhooked the 20-foot-long, thick rubber hose, 5 inches in diameter. He removed an end cap from the bottom of the milk cooler tank and connected the hose. He'd open the valve and the white gold flowed from our cooler to the truck's. Several farms' daily milk batches were collected, added to the barrel, and taken back to the dairy plant on the other side of Sauk City. Here, more testing of the entire tank was done before it was combined with other tankers full of milk. One sick cow could spoil what was already in the large stainless-steel milk cooler in our milk house. What was in our tank could spoil the entire milk carrier full and that, in turn, could affect the high-volume tanks at the dairy plant. The testing was done to ensure it was all the quality required by the FDA and/or to identify the farm that may have contaminated it. Contamination is serious and could be disastrous for the reputation of any operation.

Science is an art. If conservation is key in the fields, science is inevitable in the barn. Determining the amount of feed and minerals to be fed, consistent timing for the milking, and evaluating the quality of the milk. A farmer must be able to identify an illness that may contaminate the milk. Is the milk healthy? A farmer can see the subtleties in the color or flow and have a pretty good idea.

Life Lesson: When in doubt, toss it out.

A cow with mastitis was jumpy and sore. A cow with infection would excrete yellow or thick clumps. A cow on antibiotics meant five to seven days with unusable milk. A cow who had just given birth produced the byproduct colostrum, which was saved for the calves. In addition to the daily natural science skills of the farmer, monthly testing of the milk took place on what we referred to as "test-tube night." A small sample selected from each cow was tubed, labeled and stored for the inspector. Sometimes, the inspector was on-site to watch the operation.

Back at the dairy plant, those little plastic collection bags were also tested and recorded. Butterfat content was measured. Milk is paid at a market rate based on 3.5% milkfat. Anything above that is worth more, anything below that earns less. In 2018, the going rate paid to a farmer is $15.21 per hundred-weight or 100 pounds which equals approximately 8 gallons. The earning power for the same 3.5% milkfat per hundredweight for several years during my child-hood was:

- 1963, the year I was born: $3.50 per hundredweight
- 1970, the year I began helping in the barn: $5.03-$5.34 per hundredweight
- 1978, my first year of high school: $9.53-$11.02 per hundredweight

Prices varied based on supply and demand and other economic factors. Keep in mind that with infla-tion, $10 in 1978 is comparable to $34.78 in 2017. It's no wonder small dairy farmers are becoming obso-lete and large dairy parlors are the way of our future.

Life Lesson: Inflation does not ensure revenue.

Every two weeks, our recorded gallons, along with the count of butterfat, was totaled and the quality of milk averaged. Almost always, we tested above 3.5% butterfat—something my father was very proud of. In the summer, more cows were giving birth and we sold fewer pounds of milk. In the winter, we tried to make up for it. In 1978, we produced 60,000 pounds in our lowest month and 122,000 pounds in our highest. One might think that sounds like a healthy paycheck at about $12,000 a month. However, that is gross profit. After paying for hauling, the farm loan, insurance, and my brother's partnership paycheck, my parents were left with less than $5,000 a month. From that, they needed to pay for feed, seed corn, machinery, repairs, electricity, church tithing, and feeding and clothing our brood. We relied on beef cattle and cow sales for this very reason.

A full profit/loss statement for the Zander Family farm in 1978 showed net income of $40,000 ($175,000 revenue/ $135,000 expenses). The sale of 21 dairy cows and 42 beef cattle earned $32,000. Without the sale of animals, our income for the year would have been only $8,000 from milk production. This is equivalent to $31,758 in 2018—well below the average household income of $66,000.

My parents were smart business people, taking risks to invest back in their business to make ends meet.

Life Lesson: Farming is more than a livelihood, it's a life.

◆ ◆ ◆

ACRE 8

No Warning

My aunt lay on the couch, succumbing to weakness, high fever and nausea. Her mother tended to her fever with scraps of cloths she had wrung cold water from and placed on her forehead, while rubbing her legs from her thighs to her toes to pull the fever out of her body. It was late into the evening, when there is less cortisol in our blood. As a result, her white blood cells more readily fought the infection, which provoked more severe symptoms. Her family gathered around. Her father, her two sisters and two brothers, one of which was my father. In the first-floor bedroom where they gathered, a long, yet narrow, double hung window faced west, overlooking the barn. The family was deep in prayer, asking for improved health and survival for my aunt. Eventually, the prayers turned to survival for all seven of them. Outside of the window, they saw pieces of barn roof fly towards the house. They saw the swirling funnel cloud suddenly attacking the entire barn and surrounding buildings. The tornado was relentless as it continued toward the house. The family quickly placed their bodies over my aunt and watched in horror as the funnel cloud addressed the towering pine tree just 25 feet outside of the first-floor bedroom window. The deep tree roots would not give way to the force of the wind and debris attacking it. The loud and ferocious cloud gave up and dissipated into the night sky. They had survived the Midwest tornado of June 1934.

Life Lesson: Things can be replaced. People cannot.

Storms and ill weather can shut a farm down. The loss of buildings, equipment or even the animals themselves can be devasting to the operation. We had our share. I recall laying in a ditch to avoid a tornado and being in the safety of our basement with Alan, Cathy, Steve, and my mom, praying that Dad was avoiding a twister out in a distant field. Steve would sometimes venture to the back porch and 'storm watch' during bad weather. That made me nervous and I would beg him to come back inside. High winds, ice, snow, or even the heat from the summer sun could be damaging to buildings, animals, and the animal food storage.

Below-zero temperatures could take the life of a young calf or piglet. Torrential rains could wipe out young plants. High winds tore roofs off buildings and lightning zapped electrical equipment. Days or weeks of repairs might follow. Missing a morning or evening milking could leave cows with sour milk and udders grossly enlarged with mastitis. Timing and prioritizing repairs were of the essence.

Life Lesson: Nature deserves our appreciation and respect.

What happens when the animals are lost due to an act of God? Arising one morning in the summer of 1975, my brother Terry discovered the cows had not returned from evening grazing on the hillside pasture. A short walk around the bend took him to a devastating sight. Nineteen cows had been electrocuted by lightening as they hovered underneath a large tree for cover during a thunderstorm the night before. Dazed and confused, the few that survived were now huddled in a corner by the pasture fence line. It was a major loss for our farm. Think of this as it compares to a flood in a no-flood zone. Insurance is not always forthcoming in such situations. Fortunately, my father was a member of Wisconsin Dairies, one of the largest dairy cooperatives in the United States. Just four months earlier, Wisconsin Dairies established the Voluntary Farm Disaster Program. Funds were raised by participating producers who contributed a one-cent-a-hundredweight deduction from their milk checks. In true co-op fashion, all remaining money at the end of a year was distributed back to participating producers. My dad had participated just one month, contributing $5. Because of this fund, Do-A-Dab Farm was the recipient of a check for 75 percent of the previously recorded blended price that we would have been paid on the milk lost during the 60-day period it took to replace the herd. In addition, as any smart business person would, Dad had protected his assets and received an insurance check for $9,375, which covered approximately 60 percent of the cost to replace 19 milk-producing cows. We paid the other 40 percent out of pocket to get things back up and running.

Life Lesson: Protect your assets.

Sauk City fieldman Don Frame (left) and Ken Zander show disaster benefit check Ken received. Milk loss is based on the average of seven daily weights recorded immediately before the disaster.

'Best $5 I've spent'

"I was glad to see something like this set up," said Kenneth Zander, Rt. 1, Black Earth. "It covers a lot of things."

Ken was referring to the voluntary farm disaster program Wisconsin Dairies established last spring. It covers losses due to fire, windstorm, snowstorm, quarantine, power failure and antibiotics.

He signed up for the program and became the first producer to benefit from it.

Ken and his 22-year-old son, Terry, lost 19 Holstein milk cows on June 27 when lightening struck them during a nighttime thunderstorm.

Claim losses under the benefit program are paid with funds raised from a one-cent-a-hundredweight deduction from the milk checks of participating producers. All money remaining in the fund at the end of the year is distributed back to participating producers.

Ken's deduction for that first month amounted to about five dollars, and he received a check for 75 percent of the blend price he would have been paid on the milk he lost during a 60-day period after the thunderstorm.

"It was the best five dollars I've ever spent," he said.

Another storm was brewing. It might blow in later tonight or early tomorrow morning, but it was coming. My dad could "feel it in his bones," as he always said. Activity on our farm picked up pace every time this happened. There was limited time to get the hay stored or a field planted 'just in time.' Losing power could be disastrous to a dairy farm. The milking machines would not function and the milk cooler could only stay cool for so long without electricity. A generator could be pulled out and hooked up to keep the barn humming, depending on the length of the storm.

One night in 1981, as my father and I were nearly finished with the milking, everything came to a halt. The barn instantly darkened, and our eyes needed a moment to adjust. The machines lost pulsation and suction and loosely hung, some falling from the udders of the four cows that were being milked. Not convinced the outage would last long, my father decided that we would hand-squeeze the rest of the milk from these four cows and the remaining two with full udders. Hand milking a cow is not as easy as it looks. Proper grip is important. Dad taught me to gently clamp one teat in each hand using the thumb and first finger. Squeezing down and gently pushing the milk out by sequentially squeezing your fingers from the middle to the pinky finger. It was a tricky balance between being gentle, yet firm. My dad, with only one hand, milked four while I did one and started on a second. He took over on my second cow and we got the job done before the storm set in and power was resumed.

Life Lesson: Take responsibility, no matter what the obstacles are.

After I graduated from high school, I remained on the farm and attended Madison Area Technical College. Cathy, whom I had shared a bedroom with growing up, was now married. She, with her husband, lived in the apartment that used to be Grandma's Side of the house. Her husband, Mike Wentworth, had partnered with our brother, Terry, and our father on the farm. Cathy and Mike had been married just a month

when I awoke to Cathy pounding on my bedroom
door. Terry had just called my dad to say his wife had
been injured while taking a babysitter home. We had
been oblivious to the funnel clouds that had made
their way across what, we found out later, was 36
miles of countryside. The damage had already been
done, but the devastation was just settling in. Thankfully, there was no damage to our home or farm, so my
sister and I hopped in the car, thinking we could help.
Just two miles down the highway, we were stopped
by police and told we could not proceed. We circled
back and attempted another route but came across
similar debris—and the second story of a neighbor's
farm house, obliterated. It was here that my sister-in-
law's car was parked halfway up the 100-yard farm
house driveway—the driveway of the farmhouse she
was returning the babysitter to. After turning in the
driveway, she had seen the funnel cloud headed directly toward the car. She quickly shifted the car into
Park and stretched across the top of the babysitter
as the car windows shattered into shards of glass.
After several minutes, she sat up to see the devastation done to this local farm family's home and buildings. She and the babysitter were cut and bruised,
but alive! Had the babysitter been returned home just
five minutes earlier, her fate may have been sealed in
the rubble of her second-story bedroom, now lying in
their first-floor kitchen and across the yard.

Three miles south, my sister awoke to a horrible
rattling sound at her home in the path of the storm.

When she peered out the window, my brother-in-law, Mike, and my father were pounding on the doors and windows to alert her to the situation. She, too, had been oblivious to the devastation less than a football field away from her home. They immediately got to work attending to neighbors' horses that had lost their shelter and fencing. The next morning, we learned that the F5 tornado, known as the highest intensity rating for tornados, had killed nine people in Barneveld, just 25 minutes away, and then proceeded northeast for 36 miles, right through the village of Black Earth. We had survived the tornado of 1984, 50 years after that scary night my father and his family had been saved by the tree that still stands in the front yard of our family home.

Weather is not the only 'no-warning' zone on a farm. Farm accidents play a close second in damage of equipment, buildings, and injuries. We grew up with the constant reminder of what can happen by watching our one-armed father handled things that many with two arms struggled with. In addition, our parents often reminded us to consider 'safety first.' Looking both ways twice before crossing the road to the calf barn and pasture. Knowing the blind spots of farm equipment. The necessity of unplugging or shutting down equipment before repair and knowing the location of the hay chutes were just a few of the frequent reminders. We experienced neighbors and friends getting concussions, losing limbs, getting run over, and we even attended funerals of farm accident victims. No matter how well you practice safety, they are called accidents for a reason.

We were blessed that most of our accidents were in the form of skinned knees, barbed wire cuts, or a broken bone here and there. But we did not go without our share of close calls.

My oldest brother Terry, at the age of 45, had been a partner with my father for over 26 years. Farming was all he knew since he was a little boy, following my father from barn to tractor to field. Terry had learned all the safety rules that my parents made sure we followed. One of those involved how to interpret the temperament of the bull. Pitchfork in hand, we would release the bull from his pen and steer it down the alley with the sharp edges of the pitchfork between the bull and ourselves. Bulls have 'moods,' and when they've been penned up too long, they are dangerous animals. Terry had established an 'understanding' with his bull and could read his moods. One day, the local veterinarian arrived to help a cow through the birth of her calf. Terry knew his bull would be protective of the cow and weary of the veterinarian, so he released the bull to the cowyard just as the vet was entering the other end of the barn. The bull turned on Terry and began to charge. Terry ran for the cowyard gate and, as he began the climb over the top of it, he was head-reared by the bull and thrown through the air, landing in the sloppy manure on top of solid concrete. Terry could hear the scraping of the bull's hoofs on the cement and before he knew it, the 1,600-pound bull was pushing him across the cowyard. Twenty feet in one direction and then circled around to the other side and pushed back another 30 feet, right up against the outside wall of the barn. Terry was cornered and laid still in shock as the bull stood snorting at him. Then, the bull turned and walked away, leaving my brother for dead. Terry was coherent enough to scramble for his life and get through the entry of the barn to safety. He hosed the manure off his entire body while in excruciating pain. He suffered a few fractured ribs, a lot of bruising and some emotional scarring. The next day, a rendering service arrived. Terry could barely stand the sound he heard as the bull scraped its hooves and snorted while being loaded, onto the rendering truck. It was the end of natural mating on our farms. Terry began using the services of artificial cow semination from there on out.

Life Lesson: When you get shit on, go spray it off!

In the fall of 1985, another close call took place during an early winter snow shower. Cathy's husband, Mike, was pulling a load of cornstalks used for warm cow bedding, over the hill on South Valley Road, traveling from our home farm to Terry's place. The road was slippery from the wet snow and an early freeze that had caused the road to be icy underneath. As Mike ascended the hill on the open-air tractor, it began sliding backwards. The tractor and the chopper box it was pulling jackknifed. The tractor's front tires lifted off the road and the chopper box rolled

backwards toward the steep edge of the roadside.
Mike leaped from his seat, rolling as far as he could
from the tractor. The wagon began its descent down
the 20-foot drop into another farmers field, pulling
the tractor, which swung through the air and toppled
to the ground upside down. The chopper box landed
upright on top of the overturned tractor. All of this
happened in a matter of seconds and we were thankful Mike's life was spared. The next week, a crane crew
from Ballweg Construction strategized how to salvage the undamaged chopper box while removing it.
The tractor was able to be repaired.

**Life Lesson: Be thankful when you escape the wrath
of a storm, an illness, or an accident.**

Wentworth escapes injury

◆ ◆ ◆

ACRE 9

Give Back

A brandy Old-Fashioned—sweet or sour. The smell of cigars and pipe tobacco. The perfect Poker or Euchre hand. Cake brownies from scratch. Bowls of nuts and mints. These were all staple items at the adult card parties hosted at the Zander farmhouse for all the local farmers. Us kids were kicked out and had to be in our bedrooms at 9 p.m. The place came alive with six to eight card tables set up with ashtrays in between the players. A large pedestal ashtray was available for the stragglers and strays between games. Decks of cards laid on each table, ready to be shuffled. We may have been in our bedrooms, but we knew what was going on down there. Our private-eye spy tactics came alive. Lying on our bellies, we could peer through the radiator grates meant for the heat to rise upstairs. We could overhear the conversation, take in a ring of smoke, and even identify who had the best hand at the table.

My parents were pretty cool for their time. They were frequent hosts of card parties and other community events. For a period of time after Dad's retirement, he became a member of the Old Bastards Club. He attended the meetings at the East Side Club in Monona, just outside of Madison city limits, for the card tournaments they held. But, they were also known to have exotic dance 'entertainment.' In 2006, the club made national news for not having a stripper's permit to host such activities.

Involved and well-liked, my parents hosted sports teams and board members from various community groups, and sponsored community and political leaders. As if that wasn't enough, they were also avid community leaders themselves. They held positions on local church and community committees. My dad was, at some point, on the school board, town board, county board, Rotary, and pork producers board.

He attended many town and county board meetings as an advocate or adversary for whatever the topic at hand was. He wrote letters to the editor taking a stance on issues. He stood out in a crowd, not only with his one arm, but with his beliefs, determination, and commitment to make things better.

Life Lesson: Be a hipster!

hip·ster: *noun*

> a usually young person who is trendy, stylish, or progressive in an unconventional way; someone who is hip.
> —Dictionary.com

> *A **hipster** is someone who's eager to learn, to see—and yes—even to **do**.*

*Being a **hipster** means you're part of a subculture . . . The term **hipster** has become used rather frequently to identify anyone that doesn't appear mainstream. So, **hipsters** stand out from the crowd.*

—https://travelsofadam.com/
what-is-a-hipster/

We were active members of St. Francis Xavier Catholic Church in Cross Plains, Wisconsin, where my mom served on the church board. With strong faith, we followed all the spiritual rituals. In the spring, we'd prepare for the rising of Christ at Easter through the nine weeks of Lent, carrying out our Lenten penance. Six weeks of giving something up or committing to a service that made up for our willful wrongdoing of forsaking God or God's people. Every night during Lent, after dinner but before milking, we pulled our chairs into the front room of the farmhouse and knelt in front of them. Rosary in hand, my mom led us through the routine prayers and remembrance of the sacrifices made on our behalf. For a youngster, this was a long minute of quiet reflection. I was often fidgety and looked from brother to sister to help me brave the long chain of prayers.

In December, we'd celebrate the birth of our Savior, Jesus Christ, with midnight mass. Prior to that, my mom made sure we were strategically placed where we could not see, but only hear, the sleigh bells that represented Santa and his sleigh full of toys, being rung by my dad as he rounded the house. The tall solid wood pocket doors to the front living room, where our Christmas tree stood, had been pulled shut so that Santa could arrive unseen. My dad returned to milking and my mom took the youngest children for a drive to town to see sparkling Christmas lights and we always made a special stop in front of the Barber Sisters' home. The Barber Sisters had a nativity scene with over 100 individual pieces on display on their front porch. Beautifully lit and positioned, it was our reminder of the true meaning of Christmas.

When we arrived back home, my older siblings had finished milking and we lined up in front of those closed pocket doors, usually youngest to old-est. When Alan was 3 and I was 8, I can recall reaching across his shoulder to help him slide those doors open. The grandest sight awaited! Our aluminum Christmas tree, a type of artificial tree that was popu-lar from 1958 until the mid 1960s, sparkled. The tree featured foil needles and was illuminated from the rotating four-color wheel shining down from the cor-ner hutch.

Gifts for all eight of us, plus family games, comic books, and treats of unshelled nuts and candy were awaiting under the tree. We used that aluminum tree until 1981 when I insisted we get a real tree, for once. Now, I miss that antique tree and wish someone had kept it. I'm a sentimental ol' fool, aren't I?

We attended mass every Holy Day of Obligation and every Sunday, usually at 11 a.m. It was a tight schedule due to the morning farm tasks. Getting everyone ready and to the church on time was a chore in and of itself. Any of us who were still in the barn at 10:15 would be sent to the house to get ready and out of Dad's way. He would be in the house by 10:30 and had exactly 10 minutes to get ready. We were to be in the car by 10:45. Our kitchen clock was always set 15 minutes ahead and, at 10:50 on that clock, Mom herded us out the door to the car. Soon, Dad would join us and off we went, arriving just in time to slide into a pew before the service began.

Life Lesson: If you are not early, you are late!

The church had been built in 1874 with stone hauled by the parishioners from a quarry just four miles away. It had the traditional pointed arch entrance under the tall steeple house which held the church bells that chimed by the swinging of ropes below. The alter was beautifully crafted with the red glass candles, stained glass windows, and statues of the saints. One Friday morning, my mom drove us to the church and all that was left was rubble. The evening before, on July 20, 1972, a fire broke out and destroyed the church, burning it to the ground. The Sunday after, July 23, 1972, we attended 11 a.m. mass on the front lawn of the church, roped off with snow fence for safety. My sister, Linda, made a large plywood sign that read "THANKSGIVING IN UNITY," which stood in front of the snow fence. It represented the beginning of our fundraising efforts to rebuild our church community. My parents offered their large machine pole shed we had erected the year before as a place to hold a big fundraiser. People came from miles around to join in on Euchre tournaments, enjoy a beverage, or simply donate.

Life Lesson: Get involved!

Masses were held in the school gymnasium for 27 months. When my grandma, Theresa A. (Schmitz) Zander, passed away in August 1974, we worshipped in this gym. She was placed to rest next to her beloved husband in the St. Francis Xavier Cemetery. She was back home. In November of that same year, the dedication of the new church took place. A special mass was held where we were reminded that the church is only the frame for the parish—it is the people who worship and participate that are the unified strength. We had certainly been a part of that.

My dad was known throughout the communities of Black Earth and Mazomanie for three reasons. First, for his one-handed bowling. He frequently bowled over 200 while on the local men's league. That remaining arm was strong and the ball left his hand with power to quickly travel the bowling lane and strike the pins. Second, for his often contentious, yet respectful, letters to the editor of the local *News-Sickle-Arrow* weekly paper. He contributed frequently over the period of 20+ years. An estimation, based on averages, results in a count of approximately 800 letters in that time. To this day, I believe the newspaper sales that kept the publication alive were funded by the many locals who could not wait to see what "Kenny Zander would write about this week."

And third, but certainly not least, Dad was known for his leadership on local boards, including the Wisconsin Heights School Board. He became a board member in 1972 at the age of 41 and was elected president of the board in 1973. The *News-Sickle-Arrow* reported on the four candidates competing for two seats on the school board in 1975. Ken Zander was listed as a "challenger and vocal property tax protestor" in the article that described his beliefs and support of the local educational system, with known facts on how to minimize the associated costs. In another article, as he referred to the opposition of the recent referendum related to bussing costs, he was quoted as saying, "If you know the people of this community, I think we can get some direction."

Zander satisfied with meeting

Board president Ken Zander at the podium at last Monday's annual meeting.

He believed that the community was necessary in shaping, changing, and supporting the system, and strongly encouraged it. He was re-elected and remained president of the school board for the next three years. Running a farm while leading a school board had its challenges. My mom often accepted calls and messages on his behalf and these required my dad to conduct research and return calls during his lunch or after the evening milking. On school board meeting nights, I remember him scrambling to finish milking, get showered and dressed in his Sunday best, grab his gavel off the farm desk, and drive the 15 minutes to the school building, arriving before the 8 p.m. meeting.

Life Lesson: Keep your commitments.

◆ ◆ ◆

The Scandal

The immigrants traveled from Europe by ship, and then through the rivers and streams into the canals of Lake Erie and into Lake Michigan. Once they hit dry land, some boarded the trains and traveled by rail, while others loaded wagons with the few treasures and tools they had. The wagon train traveled across the vast land and rolling hills. Acre upon acre of hills, valleys, rocks, and the wide-open prairies that were plentiful in the 1840s. Small towns with little to no industrialization. Some immigrants had heard of Milwaukee, others of the rich soil in the Midwest. They came to pick their territory and register a claim to land by marking it with stakes. Some simply settled for a yearlong break to grow enough food, rest their horses, or fix the equipment necessary to get them to a further destination. There was no running water, no electricity, and there were no cars.

Recently, as I scoured the worn yellowed papers of the abstracts and records of sale, I discovered that the first title of the parcels of land I grew up on were recorded with the Dane County Abstract Offices in

1847. For a moment, I reflected on what I imagined life to be in 1847, before Wisconsin had even become a state! Rolling hills and miles of prairies. Sitting in a covered wagon and traveling all day to cross only 10-20 miles of the land. Stopping to build a fire for warmth or maybe rotate a small rodent over the flames for dinner. Tired and achy from the day's work of driving the horses across the rough terrain, paving the way for future generations. I imagine life living on the prairie to be like the opening scene from the TV show *Little House on the Prairie*, with children running through the tall prairie grasses and flowers. In those days, the land was untilled, and therefore allowed long distance views. Pictures and postcards from the early 1900s show bare hillsides with small trees just beginning to take root. Over the years, it was the work-up of the soil that unearthed seeds, changed the landscape and turned hillsides into small forests.

State records indicate that the first owner of what became our family's land was Jacques O'Muther. Starting with Jacques in 1847, and through 1881, our land changed owners 16 times in 34 years. Some stayed for less than a year. I suspect many of these families traveled even further west to follow hopes of mining or gold-digging. In 1881, things began to stabilize with one owner every 6-10 years.

My great-great-great-grandparents, John and Theresia Kalscheur, came to America from Germany. They landed in New York City in August 1852 on the ship called the American Ship E-Z. Their second-born son, Jacob Kalscheur, fathered my great-grand-mother, Katherine "Katie" Kalscheur, in 1868. She grew up and married my great-grandfather, Charles Karl Zander, on June 21, 1892. Katie and Charles were one pair of five Kalscheur-Zander sibling marriages.

State records indicate that the first owner of what became our family's land was Jacques O'Muther. Starting with Jacques in 1847 and through 1881, our land changed owners 16 times in 34 years. Some stayed for less than a year. I suspect many of these families traveled even further west to follow hopes of mining or gold-digging. In 1881, things began to sta-bilize with one owner every six-10 years.

On April 29, 1896, our farmland was first owned by a Zander. My great-great-uncle, Peter Zander, with his wife, named Theresia Kalscheur after her mother, one of five Kalscheur-Zander unions, purchased 80 acres with a small four-room, two-story house. Peter was my great-great-grandfather Zander's brother. Two years after buying the farm, Peter and Theresia built a new, larger farmhouse. Around this time, my great-grandfather, Charles Karl Zander, was born. Peter was 14 years older than his nephew, Charles. Eventually, Peter would deed the land to Charles and his wife, Katie (Kalscheur) Zander, who married on June 21, 1892. The next recorded document for the property isn't until 1912, when Charles and Katie contracted with the Wisconsin Telephone company in the way of a land easement to "erect poles, wires, anchors, and other appliances necessary in the conduct of its business." Together, Charles and Katie had 10 children. Their third child, Charles H. Zander, was born March 12, 1897. He became my grandpa.

My grandma, Theresa A. Schmitz, was born May 21, 1895. She grew up in Waunakee, Wisconsin, and graduated valedictorian of the Waunakee High School Class of 1912. She became a school teacher in the valley between Black Earth and Cross Plains for the Union Valley Elementary School. It was located in the field directly in front of my current residence on County Road KP, approximately one mile from the Zander Family home. This is where and how she and my grandfather, Charles H. Zander, met. He was two years younger, attending this school as one of her students. He participated in the school/community play that was casted by Theresa and held at the Union Valley School. Charles Jr. had only ever known this valley, after being raised on his family farm. My great-great-uncle, Peter, showed my grandfather how to till the land with horse and single-row plow. They milked the cows by hand and added a barn to the stable. They created our legacy that has been passed from generation to generation.

No formal recordings occur again until a series of mortgages on the property take place between 1918 and 1935. It was during this time the family scandal occurred. Charles Zander Jr. began buying the family farm from his father. A long, drawn out process. He made payments as, together, they worked the land. Today, a cigar box of checks dated between October 1918 and July 1931 show record of total payments in the amount of $18,034. Thirteen years of payments which would be equivalent to $276,137 in 2018. Think about that! A mortgage that size could take many people nearly 30 years to pay off.

But there were no land contracts or deeds to show this agreement between my grandfather and his father. They had a verbal agreement, a gentleman's handshake, as they say. When Charles Zander Jr. presented the last check to his very own father, stating, "Finally, this is my last payment and I own the farm," his father scowled at him and said "What are you talking about? You never paid a dime for the farm." Around the same time, Charles Jr. received a notice intended for Charles Sr. in the mail that his mortgage was overdue. He had no idea there was a mortgage on the land he was buying from his father. He understood his father had owned the farm outright. My great-grandfather had been mortgaging what he owned to purchase more land during the same period that my grandfather was 'buying' the property from him.

One of the mortgages shows the purchase of an additional 63 acres, making the farm a total of 143 acres in 1931. From 1900-1935, my great-grand-father borrowed money from several parties, with those parties transferring the deeds to others. These included: Henry Bowar, J.W. Ripp, Louis Westphal (beneficiary Mary Westphal), and then to Henry M. Zander in 1931 for $13,000. At one time, my great-grandfather owned almost all the Cross Plains-Black Earth Valley. The entire 13 years my grandfather was making payments, his father was using his money, along with mortgages, to purchase more land.

In the end, my great-grandfather lost everything to the mortgage holders, one of whom was his brother Henry. Henry owned the general store, the creamery and butter-making business, and most of the local bank. Henry insisted that my-great grandfather return the notes and that the property no longer belonged to either my grandparents or great-grandparents. I can only imagine my grandfather's disappointment after paying $18,034 and having nothing in return.

My grandfather persevered. After much deliberation, my grandparents made a new purchase agreement with his uncle, Henry, and purchased the farm a second time. In 1937, Henry passed and the farm became part of Henry's estate. For the next 12-18 months, it was tied up in probate while my grandfather continued to work and pay for the farm. Peter J. Zander (Henry's son) becomes executor of the estate and, in April 1939, my grandfather took on a land contract to pay the estate. July 1943 records show an executor's deed was provided to Charles H. and Theresa Zander, husband and wife, as joint tenants. It is a

fulfillment of the land contract dated April 10, 1939!
Over the course of 25 years, they paid for the farm
twice and finally owned all 143 acres!
Life Lesson: Honesty prevails.

Zander Family Farm - circa 1940

Because of this scandal, my grandfather became an
outcast to his family. His father spread rumors of his

son trying to claim the property as his own. It was one's word against the other's, since there were no formal documents other than those personal checks, which never mentioned a 'farm payment.' I'm confident that this is the reason my father believed that every agreement should be in writing. When I borrowed $1,000 from my parents to purchase my first car, I received a note showing the series of principal plus interest payments I would be making the next three years. Each month, my check number and dollar amount were recorded on this note.

Life Lesson: Financial agreements should be in writing.

My great-grandfather, who we now refer to as The Crook, passed away in early 1942 at the age of 72. His children were still at odds over the idea that their brother had tried to steal the farm out from underneath the family, thinking this to be the reason their father lost his farm. On February 9, 1942, my grandfather received a type-written note, along with a county court Receipt from Spencer A. Lucas, attorney at law in Madison, Wisconsin. It read:

Mr. Charles Zander,
Cross Plains, Wisconsin

Dear Mr. Zander:

I am enclosing check for $1.00 the amount of the bequest left to you in the will of Charles Zander. Will you kindly sign the enclosed receipt and return it to me at your convenience.

Your's [sic] truly,
Spencer A. Lucas

One final sucker punch. The check was never cashed and joined the cigar box full of cancelled checks from the initial purchase my grandfather made. For years after my great-grandfather passed, my grandmother, Theresa, carefully shared some of the facts with siblings-in-law, and they slowly uncovered the truth. Ironically, the family made amends with my grandfather shortly before he passed away from a heart attack in 1956 at just 59 years old.

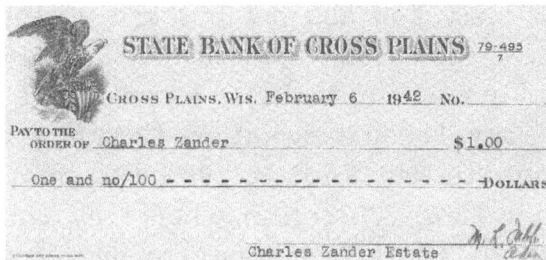

The scandal took place as my grandfather raised his family. The double purchase of the land is just one of many hardships they endured. Before there was my family, the Kenneth F. Zander Family, there was the Charles H. Zander Family: Ray, Mary Lou, Catherine,

Jeanette, and Kenny. Uncle Ray, Aunt Mary Lou, Aunt Catherine, Aunt Jeanette, and my dad. These are the relatives who shaped me.

Uncle Ray decided to purchase his own farm and moved to Deerfield, Wisconsin, about 25 miles east of his home farm. Another large Catholic family, the Raymond Zander Family became well represented in this area. They raised 13 children and I remember our family visiting them on Sundays. My Aunt Helen had a huge garden and canned everything. We ate home-made bread, drank fresh farm milk (not pasteurized), and enjoyed homemade tomato sauce, along with fresh fruit and vegetables.

All three of my aunts attended and graduated from universities, which was uncommon during the 1930s and 1940s. They were classy women and were not afraid to travel out into the world.

Aunt Mary Lou and her husband, Joseph Keating, spent their early years of marriage (1941-46) in Brooklyn, where Uncle Joe served in the United States Navy. The first two of my 12 Keating cousins were born in New York. In 1946, they moved and settled in Thorp, Wisconsin, where they owned and operated the Thorp Telephone Company for 44 years. Thorp brought them much closer to Mary Lou's family roots and visits to the Zander Family farm were plentiful and fun.

Aunt Catherine married John Gibler, and, due to travels through the United States armed services, did not visit as frequently. They would bring interesting pieces of art, including paintings, large precious stone rocks, and the famous cow cushion we all fought over.

Aunt Jeanette and Uncle Bill Olson lived in California for a while, so their visits were rare. Uncle Bill was a scientist/chemist and ended up acquiring a job for Anheiser-Busch (Budweiser) in Minneapolis, Minnesota, in the late 1960s. Their visits became more frequent. An opportunity to see them and my four 'biblical' cousins, John, Mark, Paul, and David, much more often. They loved visits to the farm. Sometimes, they would come for a weekend and one cousin would stay an entire week to help out.

On their visits, my aunts and uncles would share stories of growing up on the farm and near Black Earth. Some of their stories that stuck with me include:

> The scandal described herein. Aunt Mary Lou had great recollection of this experience and the falling out between her father and great-grandfather. She was in high school when it occurred and recalls my grandfather developing ulcers as a result. Shortly after they experienced the loss of the land and had renegotiated with her Uncle Henry, the tornado of 1934 destroyed their barn. She was hoping to go onto college and the financial impact of these events made it difficult to do so.

Life Lesson: Perseverance.

On Sundays in the summer, they often attended picnics on their own hillside. They'd pack sandwiches, fruit, and lemonade in a metal bucket to carry it up the hill. They'd invite family and friends. Together, they would gather on the hillside to rest and visit, building lasting relationships with neighbors. Those same neighbors came to their rescue in times of need, like the rebuilding of our barn after the 1934 tornado.

They recalled a time when my father was in the 8th grade and rode his bike to school. He would place the bike in a certain spot in the school yard. At the end of the day, his bike would be in another location. Little Kenny was bound and determined to find out what was going on. He began spying out the window at lunch and one day noticed a classmate pedaling his bike up the street. She had bushy hair and so, he hollered out the window, "Hey, frizzlypuss, you put my bike back!" Those were simpler times when people actually returned the items they were borrowing.

Rhubarb fever. There are two types of rhubarb fever. One happens every April, as the rhubarb would start to unfurl from the soil. This rhubarb fever was similar to spring fever. One knew that spring was really and truly on its way. Rhubarb is a delightful fruit to make pies, cobblers, sauce, and even desserts. There was a lot of it on our farm. One season, my aunt decided that rhubarb was so good, no part of it should go to waste. So, she boiled the leaves to make a soup. They soon discovered that rhubarb leaves are poisonous to the human body and act as a laxative. This type of rhubarb fever is not so kind. You know what that means. 'Nough said!

Life Lesson: Rhubarb leaves are poisonous.

Stories of wagon rides to a barn-raisings, as well as the days of horse and buggy transportation, were also plentiful. Fur coats and hand muffs, along with pails of hot coal to keep their toes warm on the ride to church.

And, of course, that fateful day in September 1950 when my father lost his arm. Hearing my Aunt Jeanette describe how she heard her brother screaming in the distance while she was picking berries, and the site of the accident as she tried to recover bits and pieces of her brother's arm, are fresh in my memory. As she told me the story, my dad sat across the kitchen table with tears running down his cheeks. This painful memory provided a special bond between the two of them and comfort in knowing that they were lucky it wasn't worse.

Life Lesson: Love prevails.

◆ ◆ ◆

Decades and Milestones

Kenneth, or Kenny, as his older siblings often called him, remained on the farm to help his parents continue farming. After that horrible accident and loss of his arm in 1950, the farm became his livelihood. He was paid $200 a month by his parents. When my parents were married in 1952, my grandpa was happy to know the farm would continue through the next generation. In 1955, he purchased another 120 acres east of the original property for $50 per acre. Total acreage of the Zander Family farm was now 263. We still fondly refer to this additional 120 acres as the Buttchen Farm, named after the family it was purchased from. After Grandpa died in 1956, my grandmother continued to own the farm until she, Theresa Zander, offered the land contract to Mom and Dad in 1960. Recently, while looking through a trunk of old pictures, I found a handwritten note tucked in the back of my great-grandmother's picture frame. My grandmother

had made a list of items and their values. This list
became the basis for a $13,000 chattel mortgage for
the purchase of tractors, cattle, pigs, and other farm
equipment. Grandma lent Dad the money to buy this
mobile capital, which he then took possession of.
When he paid her back, the animals and equipment
became legally his. The chattel mortgage was in addition to the land contract for the buildings and acreage that my dad became the owner of at about the
same time.

In 1970, before my oldest siblings were heading
off to college and careers, my father purchased another 120 acres, across Highway 14 and over the hill
on South Valley Road. Paul and Marjorie Phillips had
bought this farm in 1963 from the Padrutts, who had
owned the farm since 1914. Paul was a professor at
the University of Wisconsin-Madison and Marge was
a city girl he had married. Marge told Mom a story
about the first time she had to feed all the hired hands
who were helping on their farm. She set the table
with her good china, placing individual salt and pep-
per shakers at each setting. The farmhands entered
the warm home, removed their shit kickers and sat
at the table uncomfortably. They had no desire to
use silver and china—just give them food! Marge even
laughed at herself for her naiveite about setting the
table as if a fancy party were about to take place.
Farming was not for Marge and they ended up selling
their place to my mom and dad on land contract.

The farm grew at about the same speed as my older siblings, who were becoming young adults. Technically, the Zander Farm, as I remember it, was three farms, which we called Our Place, The Other Place, and Terry's Place. Terry remained on the farm, partnering with my father. Four other siblings ventured out into the world between 1972 and 1979 and we had three weddings within five years. Cathy went off to college and that left Alan and I to fend for ourselves. We were summoned to the barn more frequently, and thankfully my dad hired some awesome farmhands who came to our rescue.

Soon, the next generation began. Terry and Cheryl gave birth to Jason Zander and he was the first of 15 grandchildren for my parents—13 nieces and nephews for me. Our family get-togethers became larger and louder. There was always room for one more—a baby, a boy- or girlfriend, a spouse, 'adopted' siblings, a partner, and stepchildren. Friendships grew quickly amongst us.

Life Lesson: Love the ones you're with.

The hillside every one of us climbed at some point held the Indian Fort along with the picturesque view of our family farm was cherished over the years. In 1994, a group of us made the trek in celebration. We carried party hats, party poppers, balloons, and snacks in a few grocery bags and a small cardboard box. Video camera in tow, we stopped at the bottom of the hill, for a moment to discuss our plan. The group began their ascent and I took up the back of the pack and turned the video camera on. As we climbed, we shouted out things like, "Here we go," "Isn't this fabulous?" "Look at the view from here," as I turned the camera down the hill, and "I wonder where we could be going?" As we approached the Indian Fort, we began getting a bit more excited and mischievously said things like, "We are going up the hill," "We are getting close," and eventually, "Oh, look, we are at the top of the hill," "We made it!" "Oh wait! Not quite, we still have to go over the hill!" As we took our first step down the other side, we stopped and everyone grabbed a party hat and popper. Then, we all said, "Happy Birthday, Linda, you are now 'over the hill!' Happy Birthday!" It was our older sister Linda's 40th birthday and she was far away, living in Dallas, Texas, at the time. She sometimes missed our family celebrations and this was one we did not want her to miss. We continued our celebration, and, in prime time, a cargo train blew its whistle and I turned the camera on the farm with that train running beyond it in the distance. This was the view Linda loved and she had often taken photos from here while reading books on the hillside. It was the perfect celebration in her honor. After video recording our celebration, we gathered up all the party supplies, including the shreds of paper and confetti from the party poppers. Everything was placed inside the cardboard box, along with the recording. We wrapped it up, addressed it to Linda, and shipped off her 'party in a box.' I only regret not having a video camera on her end when she opened it. She described how confused she was when she opened the box and found empty wrappers and used party supplies. But then, she popped that video in and cried. I think we pulled off the perfect long-distance birthday surprise.

That was the beginning of many 'decade' birthday celebrations. The sisters started a tradition with a day or weekend get-together for each of our 40th and 50th birthdays. We celebrated with overnight trips to Chicago, Galena, St. Louis, Minneapolis, and Door County, in the Wisconsin peninsula. Over the years, we extended the invites to our spouses, with celebrations in Colorado, Napa Valley, and the Northwoods of Wisconsin at a brothers-in-law's family cabin. As our kids mature, they are also joining the celebrations. In the last 5 years, we have had six celebrations for 60th and 65th birthdays. We've rented a limousine to drive us all to a UW Badgers game, where Sharon rented the terrace at the top of Camp Randall for her husband Dan's birthday. Sharon selected a winery tour around Madison with her closest friends and family for her 60th the next year. Terry said he would prefer no celebration, but we built his 65th into a family picnic and he sure did not turn away the scratch-off lottery tickets we all loaded him up with that day! Recently, we celebrated Alan's 50th and Steve's 60th with one big celebration at Sharon's house. All our celebrations, short or long, near or far, have been amazing with adult time together to strengthen our camaraderie with, and love for, one another.

Part of our celebrations have been 'surprising' the birthday recipient with a family skit. Themes have included:

· A spoof of YMCA's "In the Navy" for my brother Steve's 50th,

· Remakes of commercials to play off the geriatric nature of products such as Depends, Preparation H, Grape Nuts, and Poligrip for Joyce's 50th,

· Customized song lyrics to "Sherry Baby" and "Shout" for Sharon's 60th, as well as "Hey Hey, We're the Monkeys," "Day by Day," and "Peggy Sue" for Linda Sue's 60th.

· And, oh, so much more

Life Lesson: Be quirky. It's 'food for the soul.'

One of our all-time favorite skits occurred locally at Brigham Park, just 12 miles south in Blue Mounds, Wisconsin. We rented a shelter and invited aunts, uncles, and cousins, along with our immediate families. The shelter was filled with family, friends, and food. We enjoyed outdoor games like Frisbee, ladder golf, and bean bag toss while wishing one of us had kept our old game of Jarts—a game with large spiked darts you threw at a hoop target placed on the ground 20 feet away. We walked to the edge of the park overlooking the Blue Mounds State Park (truly a dusty blue color) in the distance and the valleys between Blue Mounds and Sauk Prairie. It was our dad's 75th birthday. My mom insisted we perform a family skit. At this point, we had only done two or three and they weren't really a tradition yet. In good ol' Zander fashion, we established our theme and gathered our props. We wrote our script and practiced one time— only once. This has become customary for all of our skits. We find it makes them much more spontaneous and funnier.

We set the stage in the corner of the shelter with a barn made out of painted cardboard boxes and bales of straw. We took our spots and we carried off a fine production of "Hee Haw" (a popular TV show from 1969-1971) in Zander style. If you are not familiar with the show, you may wish to watch a video clip to get a feel for the hillbilly-like setting and story line. Here is the outline Cathy created and we played off of for our Zander Family version of "Hee Haw."

1. "Hee Haw" Theme Song – Hee Hee Hee Haw Haw, Hee Hee Hee Haw Haw, Hee Hee Hee Haw Haw Haw– HEE HAW! (We all come from various directions and then gather together in front of the "barn.")
2. Zander Family Salute – We'd like to salute the Zander Family, Population 10, from Black Earth, Wisconsin. Salute!
3. Old Ken Zander had a farm – e-i-e-i-o. And on that farm he had 8 kids – e-i-e-i-o. With three boys here and five girls there, here a boy, there a girl, everywhere a boy or a girl. Old Ken Zander had a farm – e-i-e-i-o.

4. Sunday Driving – We will pretend we are in a car and out for a Sunday drive after church. Alan will be Dad, the rest of us, kids. Alan will smoke a cigar (bubble gum) and we'll complain and pretend that we are getting sick. Other conversation occurs about nagging Dad to roll down his window, drive faster, and wanting to get home or stop for ice cream.

5. Sing: "Gloom, Despair, and Agony on Me," a recurring sketch-song from "Hee Haw." In it, four men in bib overalls sip from jugs, mimicking sad drunks, while they sing to country bluegrass. Each man speaks a line of the verse and they sing the refrain together.

> **Refrain**: Gloom, despair, and agony on me. Deep, dark depression, excessive misery. It if weren't for bad luck, I'd have no luck at all. Gloom, despair, and agony on me!
>
> **Verse 1**: Did you hear about those Zander boys? Why, they nearly burned their daddy's barn down. But what did old Ken do? Why, he saved those boys and the barn 'single-handedly'! (Back to Refrain)
>
> **Verse 2**: Did you hear about Ken's cows? Why, I heard they was struck dead by lightning! Nearly his whole herd was wiped out—well, at least 19 of 'em anyway! (Back to Refrain)

6. Popcorn, newspaper, and the TV – Alan will pretend that he's Dad, sitting in his favorite chair, sleeping with his popcorn and newspaper. There will also be a TV on. One of us will come up and turn the channel. Dad will wake up and tell us to turn the channel back—he's watching that!

7. Cornfield Pop-ups, another famous "Hee Haw" sketch – We'll pop up and tell several jokes, such as, "Hey, how high is the corn?" and the rest of us answer "Why it's knee-high by the 4th of July!" Other jokes?

8. Finale – Each kid will do our own family salutes. Each of us will step forward and say our individual family name, population, where we live and a salute to Dad. After each we all holler, "Salute!"

We slapped our knees and danced in do-si-do fashion and laughed at our own crazy antics. As you can see, we like to have fun and we like to share memories. Our family experiences, our relationships, and the memories and traditions we've created are an important part of our legacy.

Life Lesson: All that truly matters in the end is that you truly loved and are loved.

How do you preserve a legacy? My dad was always looking for a way to do so and preparing for the future. He established the farm partnership with Terry and added in my brother-in-law, Mike. As the two of them began to take over many of the farm responsibilities, my father ventured into property management of two duplexes. These would be an opportunity for revenue to begin setting aside for his retirement fund. He also began selling for Hughes Hybrids, a corn seed company. These were ventures that helped him remain actively involved in the farming community. He became involved with government officials regarding local land use and advocating for farmers' rights. Since land-use and zoning regulations often restrict the rights of owners to use their property as they otherwise could (and want to), they are, at times, controversial. The bottom line for my dad was to advocate for land owners and the ability to make decisions on how to utilize their own land.

While writing this book, I spoke with a few family members who had their own discussions with Dad on land use. I learned he had often asked for insight from us and looked out for our futures at the same time. For example, before venturing into land conservation with the Natural Heritage Land Trust (now Groundswell Conservatory), he had several conversations about the approximately 80 acres on the far end of the farm. He drove my brother-in-law, Dan, around the fields in the golf cart-like Kawasaki Mule. They discussed whether this piece of land might be good for a countryside golf course. In the end, he decided against it. Today, it is part of the land trust, a nonprofit, community-based organization that conserves land by permanently protecting it from development. I share it with my friends for hiking and snowshoeing.

Another time, he reached out to my niece, Tanya, and her husband, Mike Goth. Dad had identified a piece of land near Sauk City, 15 miles north of Do-A-Dab, that he heard was for sale and thought it might be a good investment for them due to the location and quality of land. They were looking for a place to build a home and allow for expansion of Mike's plumbing business. As a young couple, they were unable to afford the land and, in the end, passed on purchasing it. In 2016, the land became the site of the Sauk Prairie Hospital along Highway 12 on the north side of Sauk City.

We often reflect on the foresight my father had. Yet, the best preservation of a legacy is stories passed from generation to generation. I encourage the grandchildren of Kenneth and Charleen Zander, listed here in the order they were received by the Zander Family, to pass along these stories of hardships, kinships, and relationships to future generations. I love you all!

Jason Zander

Jessica Vils

Tanya Zander

Amanda Benzine

Travis Vils

Kimberly Zander

Jamie Wentworth

Ashley Benzine

Hayes Hoessel

Nichole Wentworth

Jeremiah Kalsow

Stefani Higdon

Ryan Kalsow

Chelsea Bridge
Casey Bridge

◆ ◆ ◆

ACRE 12

The Letter

The Royal typewriter sat on the industrial metal desk just inside the front door of our farmhouse. A manual beast compared to today's technology. One piece of paper inserted and aligned into the dual rubber rollers of the typewriter carriage. An inked roll of ribbon running from one spool to the other as it moves through the threader to lift it into place with the stroke of each key. After typing one line of text, a bell rings and you raise your left hand to the manual return bar and slide the whole carriage to the right.

My mother, the sole farm accountant, used this machine to pound out the farm bookwork in neatly aligned rows of numbers, along with descriptions of each entry. The front porch was like Grand Central Station with eight children, farmhands, my father, and area farmers and vendors stopping by. So, she often did her bookwork in the evening after we had settled into bed. The keys of the typewriter took finger strength to press hard enough for the metal letter to make it from the internal organ of the typewriter through the ribbon and onto the paper. Especially if the ribbon was being recycled a second time through the machine to save money. It was difficult to type 50 words per minute on a machine like this, much less the 80-100 many can do today on their computer keyboards. Each key needed to be pressed with purpose. If you pressed a key too softly, the arm would raise but the letter would not hit the paper. You needed a firmer, longer strike. Each strike required steady pressure to get the letters typed evenly. Sometimes, a half letter appeared, and you had to backspace and try that letter again. Thus, the long nights my mom sat at this machine.

For those of you unfamiliar with such an antique you can learn more here: *ww.explainthatstuff.com/typewriter.html*

Over the years, we each took our turn with the machine, pounding out memos, attachments, addendums, book reports, and other pieces of homework. My history reports often included citations and footnotes directly from our full-volume Britannica Encyclopedia set. A luxury many farm children did not have and another item that is nearly obsolete in today's world, replaced with the more simplistic Google search.

More importantly, the typewriter was used to capture purpose and insight to and for our local community. Over the years my father, a vocal local, crafted hundreds of letters to the editor and documents to submit to a variety of county and state entities with his thoughts on human rights, local rights, and farmer's rights. He spent hours putting words to paper with pen to share lessons, encourage perspective, and make lasting impressions. Each letter was meticulously crafted using his remaining left hand, which he had taught himself to use after his accident. The letters were sometimes squiggly, and the paper was often found with scratched out re-writes. He would then hand this to my mother and she would type it out to send to the audience it was meant for.

Life Lesson: Stand up for your beliefs and educate others along the way.

Recently, I came across an example of perspective he was sharing with our combined townships of Black Earth and Mazomanie, which shared the Wisconsin Heights School District. It had been years since he was school board president and since any of his own children, or even some of his grandchildren, were in high school. A few grandchildren, including my two sons, were still representing our family, but my father never passed up an opportunity to make a difference for anyone and everyone. Here is an example from 2006 of the messages he would use to foster others to think about and to represent what mattered to him.

Letter to the Editor,

Within the past week I have seen two different talk shows about a young woman who was a geographic reporter. Her

*name was Lisa Ling. She was telling how she wanted to do
an article on North Korea but found out they did not allow
an American in to their country and no one was allowed
to come in with a camera.*

*Lisa was a friend of a famous cataract eye surgeon (not
American) who went to Korea periodically to do eye sur-
geries. The two of them agreed on telling the Korean
leaders that this surgeon would not come unless he could
bring along his medical advisor which happened to be an
American (Lisa). After a period of time they did agree to
this stipulation thinking that Lisa was a medical advisor
even though she knew nothing medical.*

When they arrived they found that:

1. *4 or 5 armed escorts would be with them 24 hrs. a day
   not to protect them but to watch them so they did not
   go anywhere they didn't want them to;*
2. *No cell phones were allowed in North Korea;*
3. *No phone calls could be made out of the country or into
   the country. They were completely isolated from the
   rest of the world and from their families for the dur-
   ation of their stay, which Lisa said was very scarey*
   (sic)
4. *Only TV or radio stations run by the government are
   seen or heard by the people of North Korea and they
   are only told what the government wants them to
   hear. Many of these people think the war with the
   United States is still going on today because that is*

what they are told;

5. *The people can only congregate to honor their leaders and can never speak against them. If someone does, they just seem to disappear;*

6. *Lisa did smuggle in a camera but only got a couple of pictures inside homes of cataract patients.*

How sad this does seem!
How lucky we are here in America!

We can have cell phones, can call anywhere in the world, we have computers, cars, toys, basically we can have or do almost anything possible if we are willing to work for it. What a great country we live in. We have access to hundreds and probably thousands of TV and radio stations that are not run by the government. We can speak to or about anyone we want to (as long as it is not libelous). It appears we can even have radical professors with warped minds who teach at our universities and also other people who call our leaders every name under the sun and then call them liars and accuse them of orchestrating 9/11 and blowing up the trade center to gain power, and guess what, these people can do this because they are protected just like you and I and everyone else under our Constitution of the United States of America regarding free speech. Can you imagine what would happen to these people in a country with a dictator such as North Korea?

And then after I finished watching these shows I picked up the News-Sickle-Arrow and read the article on the front page. It appears as though we are back to square one where the administration only wants certain board members and the public to know what they want them to know. To the best of my knowledge, school board members are elected by the residents of the district to represent them by being fiscally prudent to provide the best education possible for the children. The law, rules, and regulations for open meetings law are pretty much guided by the State and board members take an oath of office upon being elected. The board responsibility is to set policy and hire administration to carry out these policies. If the administration fails to do this they should be replaced. It appears that under the previous administration many of these policies were changed so that the administration was in control over the policies and over the board.

When it gets to the point where a board member needs permission from the board president or the administrator to speak to another board member we are getting close to a dictatorship. It appears as though someone is trying to hide something.

Soon the board wants a referendum to exceed spending limits. Of course it was already in the paper that a $200,000 valuation would probably result in an extra $500 in taxes each year for three years. What they did not tell you is that this would probably be the lowest amount and that farmers could pay 5 or 6 times that much, based on their valuation. This could amount to $7,000 or $8,000 additional taxes over 3 years. I think there *are many people who cannot afford this kind of luxury for this school district. Maybe a better approach for the school board would be to make better management decisions and be a little more frugal in handling the taxpayer's dollars (something that should have been started under the previous administration when there was so much squandering of the taxpayer's money).*

Think about it.
Kenneth F. Zander

Controversial? Yes. My father was not afraid to state political opinions, controversial statements, or emotional topics. He believed and accepted that there were different perspectives, but he always spoke about his reasons and the difference of opinions because he also believed others needed to hear the facts, realities, and perspectives to make their own educated decision. In fact, after he passed, our local editor wrote his own editorial about my dad.

John's Journal
By John Donaldson

It may go without saying that the late Ken Zander and I disagreed about a lot of things. What may come as a surprise to many, however, is that we found lots of common ground too.

When I first met this brash dairy farmer with a hook on one arm and a clenched fist on the other, my first thought as the local long-haired reporter/editor was that the school board meetings were going to be getting very, very interesting, not to mention longer.

The '70s, as now, were tough times financially, and the Wisconsin Heights School District was grappling with the issue of what to do with its dilapidated elementary school buildings. There was a whole series of referendum losses, with a strong contingent in the villages holding firm that the district needed to rebuild two K-8 buildings and keep the kids in their home communities.

I didn't think that made sense, and initially I was surprised to learn that Ken Zander didn't either. We agreed that duplicating all those services and grade levels, year after year, would cost the district millions. We also both agreed, when the time came, and a two K-8 referendum was finally put forward, that we needed to hold our noses and vote for it because that was the only way anything was going to get done. Those old buildings were seriously unsafe.

When I thought about it more, I came to realize I shouldn't have been surprised. Ken, after all, was a farmer raising a herd of kids out on the eastern edge of the school district. Bussing wasn't an issue to him, it was a fact of life. Yes, he thought that combining kids by grade level would save money and perhaps even lower property taxes a little, but he also knew that extra money would also mean extra resources for kids. Ken Zander liked kids and always wanted to do what he thought was best for them. Obviously, not everyone agrees on the definition of "best," but if your heart is in the right place, that's a step in the right direction.

Ken's heart was in the right place at all times. He was a man with strong convictions, yet a man capable of listening to the opinions of others. Sometimes, he even allowed himself to be swayed by those opinions. Other times, he was willing to take a position he didn't necessarily like because it was the only way to get the job done for kids. It's getting harder and harder to find politicians like that anymore.

Over the past couple of weeks, I've probably been asked a hundred times how I'm going to fill the large hole on my editorial page, references to Ken's frequent letters to the editor. The other day Ken's widow – cracking a wry smile – asked me if she was supposed to start writing letters now.

I'm not too worried about a lack of letters, but I'm always sad to see a prolific letter-writer pass on. Letters to the editor, in my opinion, are lifeblood for a community newspaper, and Ken Zander was a frequent donor. His down-home style and his topic selection never failed to illicit a reaction, and that, from an editor's point of view, is good for business. Discussion begets more discussion, and pretty soon, ideas start bubbling to the surface. Some of them are good ones.

Shortly before he went into the hospital, Ken came into my office to talk, as he often did. I think he liked the idea my reading a letter in front of him so he could gauge my reaction. This time, however, he brought no letter. He just wanted to talk. He congratulated me on my daughter's accomplishments in school, and we talked about his approaching surgery. I could tell he was nervous about it... Who wouldn't be? We probably spoke for half an hour, then he waved goodbye and headed down to the café to talk some more.

These were the last of many, many conversations. Some were heated, others were laced with laughter, but all were conducted with a great degree of mutual respect. You could disagree with Ken, but you had to respect him. He earned it.

Life Lesson: Make a difference.

As John mentions, my dad was a frequent contributor to the local *News-Sickle-Arrow* weekly paper, writing on behalf of the communities and counties in the area. There was one letter that he wrote that was meant for one person and one person only. This letter was not submitted to the paper or any local officials.

This letter mattered more than any other he had written. THE Letter. It remains in the squiggly, purposeful handwriting of my father. In the wee hours of the morning of my parent's 49th wedding anniversary, he sat at the vinyl cloth-covered kitchen table and crafted these words:

Dear Char, Toots, Mom

These are all of my favorites! It is early in the morning and I woke up thinking about the last 49 years. Forty-nine years looking ahead seems so long, yet looking back at the 49 years of our marriage seems so........ short.

We have shared good times and bad times together. I believe the good times have overshadowed the bad by far and hope you feel the same!

The day I lost my arm I thought my life ended but then God rewarded me with a jewel. Her name was Char! Little did I realize at the time just how big a jewel you were. But day by day that jewel becomes bigger and brighter.

When we took our vows 49 years ago for rich or poor – sickness or health I don't believe we really understood what that meant. In our case God has given us the richness and the health. How lucky we have been! The richness of our nine children, eight healthy and able, and one as an angel to watch over all of us, and our health with no major problems so far. Hopefully this will continue for many more years.

As you probably know by now that I never was much for this public mushie love stuff. This does not mean I don't love you because I do. It only means that I could have and should have told you much more often. I would find it very hard to live without you, Dear. You are my life! Thank you for the 49 years of happynes (sic) *that you have given me! Hopefully we have many more to come.*

This is to tell you I love you and happy 49th on this May 28th 2001.

My anniversary gift to you!

> *Love,*
>
> *Ken*

P.S. luv ya!

This letter is a treasured gift my mom has shared with all her children and grandchildren. We all re-read it from time to time.

Life Lesson: Write letters. Especially love letters. Say "I love you."

❖ ❖ ❖

ACRE 13

An Auction

The boardroom at State Capitol Credit Union, my place of work in Madison, was on the third floor overlooking an office park. Today's training topic was Managing Change. The facilitator opened with an exercise: think of a change you have experienced and how you managed it. I loved this stuff. I am good at accepting change. I am resilient. I know how to push through and I am proud of it.

It was my turn to share and so I began. "Four years ago, the place where I grew up, my family farm, was auctioned off." *Sigh.* "Some cows, some machinery, a lot of equipment." *Gulp.* "Buildings not in use deteriorated quickly and so, we had already torn down the barn." *Lip quiver.* "And outbuildings." Eleven faces peered at me. A voice in my head said, "So what, who cares?" The emotions began boiling and, within 20 seconds, I erupted. I was in tears. I pushed my chair back, stood up, and quickly exited the room. Maybe I hadn't managed this change as well as I thought. Oh sure, I was resilient. Resilient in blocking out my feelings up until this point. I pushed through at the time, but today I was going to have to face those emotions.

"Nothing is so painful to the human mind as a great and sudden change."
—Mary Wollstonecraft Shelley, from Frankenstein

Like a flood, it all came rushing back.

That dreary day brought with it the bleakness of the task at hand. Early spring, yet winter was still in the air. Dressed in our winter coats, we pulled machinery out of the storage shed and lined it up in the field outside the farmhouse's large picture window. We loaded boxes of tools and miscellaneous pieces of farm equipment onto flatbed wagons. An old hand plow and rusted milk cans reminded us of the history already made and nostalgia set in. How could we let this go? It was more than just stuff—it was our stuff. The tractor I carried lemonade to, the pitchforks and shovels I used to clean and maintain the barn, and the mill I had unloaded countless gravity wagons of corn into. I wanted to buy it all, but here we were. Day of sale: March 11, 2005.

Life Lesson: Memories are more important than possessions.

The Bill Stade Auction & Realty Company auctioneer truck pulled into the driveway. Locals came from miles around and parked on the side of County Road KP, as well as Moen Valley Road. They began gathering 'round, inspecting sale items and strategizing how they would bid on their picks. My dad stepped over to the two auctioneers and conferred on the order the items would be open for bid. Our large circle driveway once again coming in handy to move the auctioneer truck to each 'stage' around the farm. The auctioneer's assistant raised the large garage door-type window in their camper like truck bed and began to assign paper numbers to bidders. It didn't take long for the bidding to begin. "Who will start with $100 for this air compressor? Here! $120? Yup! 140? Here!" The bidding continued throughout the day, various arms waved their auction numbers through the air while the auctioneers tracked the offers. "Going once, going twice . . . Three times and SOLD!"

When all was said and done, the items auctioned off that day provided $117,166 towards retirement for my mom and dad.

The auction brought peace to my dad. He no longer had to worry about who would take over or how they would survive in a profession that was difficult to make ends meet. It also brought finality to his career. A very late retirement at the age of 74.

His retirement preparation had begun many years prior. By attending local and county board meetings, he had learned the process for rezoning property. He began looking at options for selling part of his beloved farmland as residential lots. All in all, there were seven lots ranging from 4-11 acres each. Together, he and I walked the four parcel edges containing 26 acres that were recently rezoned. Parts of a field here, a wooded hillside there. My dad shared his internal struggle with the decision. 'Chunking up' the farm was hard. He was nearing retirement and, although my oldest brother had partnered with him to run the farm, it was a commitment too big to carry on alone. Larger farms were taking over the small family ones. Milk prices were low, feed prices high, and farm equipment expensive. Then, my dad stopped, looked to his left, into my eyes, and then out at the valley and wept. He wept for the change occurring, wept for the memories of working this field for 60 years of his life. Wept out of happiness that my husband and I could purchase a piece of this land and continue to thrive off it. We commiserated together for a little bit and then got to work on drafting up our land sale agreement with my husband. It was a bittersweet moment and provided an even stronger bond between the two of us.

In 1998, when Dad stopped milking at the home farm and moved the best cows to our second dairy barn at Terry's place on the other side of the highway, our main milking barn was razed. Initially, it was dismantled, board by barn board, to salvage the best wood, which was sold to a furniture company to make 'rustic, authentic, antique' furniture. Each of my siblings was given an opportunity to purchase something made from our own barn wood. A kitchen table, a bookshelf, a nightstand, and picture frames are all that remain in the family from our barn. With the wood gone, the cement was crumbled and crushed, and the ground was leveled. My parents built their retirement home right where the barn had been.

Soon after that, my father was one of the first in the area to consult with the Natural Heritage Land Trust, now known as Groundswell Conservancy, about protecting the remaining farmland. This countywide non-profit organization provided an intentional usage agreement with contractual stipulations in exchange for payment. The farmer or land owner continues to own the land, but has limits on how it can be used and maintained. This conservation easement sealed the deal on Dad's eligibility to retire.

The auction was simply the culmination of all his prep work. It was the end of his farming career and the official beginning to retirement. He had secured a strong financial position for him and my mother just in time.

Life Lesson: Change is inevitable. The only thing constant is change itself.

Life is a series of natural and spontaneous changes. Don't resist them; that only creates sorrow. Let reality be reality. Let things flow naturally forward in whatever way they like.
—Lao Tzu

◆ ◆ ◆

ACRE 14

Life Changer

"What the hell just happened?" I asked. I was at my parent's home as the sun was peaking over the horizon, ready to brighten the day. My mother sat on her end of mauve, cream, and blue patterned couch, next to the end table with the lamp and Bose radio. I was on the other end, where the grandfather clock began its quarter-hour chime—5:45 a.m. The previous four weeks haunted our thoughts. At 11:30 p.m. the night before, we had been summoned to Madison. Thirty minutes of worry as my brother-in-law solemnly drove my sister, myself, and my mother in my sister's red Chevy Trailblazer. Several months before, I had meandered through the late-night entry to the Madison Meriter Hospital emergency room to stay with my husband after his back surgery. Now, I navigated my brother-in-law to the closest parking area and directed our group to the entrance. From there, we scuttled through the sterile hallway to the bank of elevators waiting to lift us to the intensive care unit. My heart remained on the first floor while my head forced

me to take a series of footsteps on floor six until we
arrived at the large, double-wooden doors with a self-
assist entry. Hesitation. There was no turning back.
Did I want to go in? Did I need to go in? Why not turn
on my heels and run the other way? Or should I burst
through in hope? Like robots, we pushed the doors
open and searched for an answer to why we were here
at this ungodly hour.

It was hard to tell the time of day in the ICU. Patient rooms were in various states of activity. The
tabs of different colored plastic flags near the door
outside of each room—a red, white, yellow, or green
flag swung toward the front, identifying what the
person behind the curtain needed in the moment.
Nurses running with an IV stand or dragging a mobile
vital sign monitoring unit as they made their rounds
from room to room. Further in the distance, a doctor walking towards us, knowing we belonged to Ken
Zander. Behind us, my siblings trickling in after being
awakened to the news.

My dad had taken a turn for the worse. A second
cardiac arrest after his open-heart surgery. The surgery that was meant to prolong his life. He survived
the first. *We* survived the first. He had been placed in
an induced coma after a pacemaker was installed to
allow his body to recover from his heart stopping and
being pounded back to life again. Father's Day 2007
was one for our family history book. We celebrated
in the hospital's family room, taking turns to visit
the room where my dad was intentionally drugged

to rest. There were too many of us. Eight children and those we had chosen to start our own families with. Seven of the fourteen grandchildren had joined in. The family waiting room was the place we used to celebrate OUR father. After lunch, we gathered outside of his ICU room for a family picture, a bold sign hanging over us, "Intensive Care Unit." As if anyone could forget where we were. Later that day, the doctors and nurses encouraged us to set up a visiting schedule, which we did. I now had to wait my turn to see my dad. I guess one could think this was no different than the rest of my life—he was busy and there were eight of us, after all. Little did the hospital staff know, my dad never thought there were too many of us. Never.

Blessed indeed is the man who hears many gentle voices call him father.
—Lydia Maria Francis Child

Here we were again, minus those who had traveled back to their homes outside of or across the state after that Father's Day celebration. Tonight, we were staring at the doctors walking toward us and stopping dead in our tracks to hear the voices and machines at work. "Clear!" *Pause. Pause. Pause.* "Heart rate flat!" The long piercing scream from the machine telling us it was over. "I'm sorry, there was nothing else we could do." Or something to that effect, because it doesn't really matter what anyone says or does in those moments. Numbness sets in.

Behind the curtain, we know he awaited. Waiting

for us to say goodbye, waiting for the Good Lord to take him home. The Our Father prayer gave us strength as we watched my mom hold his hand and remind us he was in a better place. He had endured a life of hardship and pain. He had lived, loved and laughed through it all. He had surely experienced the deepest love known to mankind with my mother by his side. On June 27, 2007, at 1:33 a.m., at the age of 43, I said goodbye to my 76-year-old father. Life would never be the same.

Life Lesson: *To say goodbye is to die a little.*
—Raymond Chandler, The Long Goodbye

I sat on the front porch of the home my husband and I had built on six acres of the original Zander Family farmland. Curled up like a cat on my husband's lap on the rocking chair. My body shaking with uncontrollable sobs and gasping for air. Life would never be the same. I walked the valley roads that connected the patchwork of fields. A neighbor hopped off his tractor to console me. Life would never be the same. I recalled the combine rides my two sons took with their grandpa, leaning up against the glass panels watching the machine gobble up the corn.

Ryan (inside) and Jeremy Kalsow picking corn with Grandpa

Life would never be the same. I wrote down things I didn't want to forget, such as how his eyes lit up when I walked in the room and the large bowls of popcorn he consumed as a snack. Life would never be the same. I recalled the Hershey candy bars he shared with me after my older siblings boarded the school bus in the morning. Life would never be the same.

The memories came rushing back, but I wanted the real thing. I didn't want to forget and I thought I would.

re·sil·ience: *noun*
an ability to recover from (or adjust easily) to misfortune or change.
—Merriam-Webster.com

Another lesson in resilience. My dad had done it when he lost his arm, my mom when she lost a baby, and as a family, we had pushed through life experiences that mattered. This would be the true test of how well I had learned from my parent's demonstration of resilience. Adjust easily? Nope. Recover? Eventually.

As nearly a thousand visitors payed their respects at St. Xavier Catholic Church, the satin lining in the lid of the casket represented his livelihood. A screen-printed picture of the farm tucked in the valley that runs between the rolling hills of southwest Dane County, Wisconsin. His life represented on a piece of fabric as it had already been imbedded in his heart. The land my father, his father, and his grandfather before, had walked, tilled, planted, and harvested. This picture brought some life back to the casket. He and his legacy would be laid to rest so that he could continue to enjoy the view, knowing the real legacy was still beating in us.

Life changer. Not only was my dad's passing my most life-changing event ever, my dad was a Life Changer. Nine hundred seventy-eight people sat in the pews of the same church our family had helped rebuild. They waited their turn to pay their respects. When summoned, they walked past the picture boards of his life. Past the carefully selected flowers. No lilies—my dad was allergic to them or despised their scent to the point of an illusion of an allergy. Nine hundred seventy-eight people paid their respects to my father before entering the long line to share their sympathies with a family still in shock.

Sharing stories of his tenacity, his impact, and his ability to bring the best out in others. There were eight of us, and our spouses, and our children, and, in some cases, our children's spouses. We stretched the length of the church's main aisle and anyone who had made it through that whole stretch had given us over an hour of their time. Many of them with their own aching hearts, loving him as much as we did. We all come into this world with family and leave it with family. In between, you make your own family. My dad understood the more modern definition of family before anyone defined it. A group of people, usually of the same blood (but do not have to be), who genuinely love, trust, care about, and look out for each other. You can't take things with you, but experiences and people become part of our soul. They remain with us in our spirit.

Nancy and her Dad on her wedding day - 1985
Life Lesson: Be a life changer.

ACRE 15

Ties that Bind

Oh, that next year after Dad's death and, at times, still. We reminisced, cried, found signs that Dad was with us, and grew in appreciation of the legacy our dad had built. We became closer as we supported Mom in all the 'firsts' without Dad. I am blessed with a large family who cares about each other. We never have to look for love. It is unconditional. It is hard for my siblings and I to imagine those who don't have relationships like we have developed. Yes, developed! Our strong family values taught by our parents as we experienced them first-hand while growing up are certainly behind our willingness to accept and forgive one another. We have a strong bond. The summer after Dad passed, we planned a weeklong family vacation and rented a house in Frisco, Colorado. One house. We have a strong bond, but not that strong. It's separate housing from now on!

If Mom has said this once, she's said it a thousand

times. Each time she was pregnant, she would hear re-
marks such as, "Not another one," and "That is a lot
of kids (a.k.a work)." Today, she says, "I'm the lucki-
est woman in the world to have all of these helping
hands. All those people who wondered what I was
doing back then underestimated the value of family.
It's payback time!" What goes around, comes around.
Every single one of us plays our role in keeping Mom
young, healthy, and social. She doesn't need much
help with any of them, but she is taking advantage of
it.

Admittedly, relationships of any kind require
work. And we Zanders know how to work! That was
life lesson number one! So, together, we turned the
splotch of land where the pig barn once sat into a memorial garden. My mom can see the garden from her
living room window. My husband prepared the land
and collected native prairie flower seeds. We added
some trees to surround the garden and placed a bench
at its far end. When sitting in that bench, you overlook the property and the farmhouse. It is peaceful
and beautiful. Periodically, a biker stops to eat a picnic lunch. The garden is marked with a barn-shaped
wooden sign crafted by my husband. The sign simply states, "*Kenneth F. Zander* Memorial Garden." My
husband surprised my whole family by scroll-sawing
my father's proportionately enlarged, scratchy, handwritten signature out of wood and placing it on the

sign.

Our significant others and spouses are warmly welcomed and many of our friends become 'adopted siblings' if they choose. They join us in our get-togethers, take turns hosting us, and even join in our family
skits. As adults, we get together and *klatsch*. The term
is German for "informal discussion or gossip." It's
hard to explain what this sounds like, but you know
what I mean if you come from a large family. Imagine
about six conversations at the same time, each competing for space on the air waves. One brother-in-law
describes it as a bunch of chickens, cackling loudly as
they scramble to compete for the kernels of corn on
the ground. I suppose it is, as our voices get louder and
more enthusiastic and each conversation eventually
ends in an outburst of laughter.

Because we can be overwhelming for some, the in-laws sometimes refer to themselves as "the outlaws." We lovingly support their need to make peace with our absurdity and accept that they are truly part of the whole. We'll call them whatever they want, but they are part of the ties that have kept us together.

We can go weeks, months, or even years without

seeing one another, but like my brother, Steven Leo, told me once, "If any one of us needed something, the others would be there." That proved true when Cathy lost her husband after complications from his third open heart surgery and again when Steve suffered several strokes.

Life Lesson: Family is forever!

◆ ◆ ◆

ACRE 16

Relish in the Moment

L ife goes on. Seasons change. Winter, spring, summer, fall. We are blessed with four very differently weathered seasons in Wisconsin. Each bringing a reminder of change, growth, restart, or simply the same joys and challenges of a similar season in the past. A change of colors, or temperatures, or weather are often used to describe it. We laugh and say, "If you don't like the weather in Wisconsin, just wait five minutes and it will change." It can be erratic and sporadic. Farming is a profession controlled by the weather and each seasonal change provides the necessary ingredients for the cycles of growth, renewal, fuel, and rest.

Winter is often the season to rest and catch up. It's a time to repair or service equipment that the other seasons take their toll on. Days are shorter and the farmer also gets a bit more rest. In winter, using the stored food for both the animals and the family lightens the daily routine to milking, cleaning, testing, and repairing. Bitter cold seeps through the wooden doors of the barn and storage sheds. The animals provide the only heat. The barn is much more inviting in the winter—a reprieve from the snow and cold. In the house, our radiators provide warmth from the raw outdoors and are a great place to place mittens, socks, and boot liners to keep them warm and dry for our next outdoor adventure. The snow, cold, and consistent dairy farm daily routine keeps the farmer busy as he awaits spring planting.

Spring—everything unfurls—the frost, the leaves, the mice and the weeds. Soon, it is time to prepare the field for the seeds that provide nutrition for the rest of the year. Plowing to overturn the soil, disking to break it up into smaller chunks, and then raking it to even it out. We might load up on a flatbed wagon and be sent to pick up rocks that had surfaced during this process. This is the time of year that machinery is oiled and prepped for the upcoming planting and fieldwork.

Summer is crop growing season. Fertilizing the crops at the right time and with the right nutrients. Cultivating between the rows to ensure the roots of the plants are not overtaken by weeds. As the crops get bigger, a handpicking of some invasive plant may be needed. I remember the yellow mustard plant. Was it invasive? Or did Dad need something to keep us busy? We would spend hours picking the yellow plant out of the alfalfa fields. Fresh-cut alfalfa is baled and thrown from baler to wagon, making hay for the cows to eat. It is manual labor from the wagon to the elevator, where the bale was hoisted into the hay mound in the barn. Up in the barn, two or four more hands meticulously stacked the bales to ensure adequate storage space.

Fall harvest. It is here the farmer reaps the rewards of many hours of his labor. Did Mother Nature cooperate, applying the right combination of sun and rain? If so, the harvest will be plentiful. The combine and chopper are put to work to collect the fruit and stalks from the crops. Corn and soybeans need a certain moisture (or lack of) to be safe enough to store. Otherwise, the heat of a silo, along with the moisture, could start a fire.

Life is like the changing seasons and our Wisconsin weather—wait five minutes and it will change. There are seasons of birth, fun, growth, love, learning, renewal, pain, sadness, maturity, and death. Just as we don't have much control over the changing of the seasons, we often don't have control of when we experience life's ruts, or have a conflict with our workplace, community, or country. Accepting change allows you to take advantage of what the 'season' has to offer while preparing for what is yet to come.

The average human life span of 79 years is just a nanosecond of time in this vast world of ours. We fight the seasons or try to beat them. Wishing we could wear shorts in winter or drive a car before we are legal driving age. Wishing we were married with children when we are dating. Wishing we did not have to work so we could travel more or that we did not have to travel for work. How ironic that we are always wishing for what we do not have today or what we used to have. Why not relish in our moments on this Earth?

Aunt Jeanette, my dad's sister and my godmother, is the one who taught me how to 'relish.' It was her version of what is today called 'mindfulness.' The ability to pay attention to everything the senses can take in, grasping them in your awareness until they are embedded in your heart. When you are at peak awareness, you become alert and capable of feeling, hearing, and seeing things that can easily be bypassed otherwise.

Life Lesson: Learn to relish.

Stop. Take it all in. Do nothing but breathe. It is 86 degrees and 93% humidity as I write this. Breathing is difficult in this thick air and I could easily move back to the comfort of my kitchen table in the air-conditioned house my husband and I built on six acres of my family farm. But it is here, on my front porch, overlooking the valley, where the words begin to come to me. Almost spiritual, in a sense. A different type of comfort. I feel Dad by my side. And here I am, crafting a legacy of my own, after his legacy. The changing seasons of the circle of life.

Look. What do you see? The landscape is the same, yet different. Today, the green grass and sunshine are intense. The corn in the field across from me is already waist-high, though we have four days until the infamous 'knee-high by the Fourth of July' adage is due. Bike riders are pedaling past—they come here for the hills and thrills. In the distance, beyond the silos of our neighbor's farm, there is a haze—that summer mirage making the landscape look warped and wrinkled. It changes the perspective of the view.

Listen. What do you hear? Birds. So many birds singing and chirping and tweeting. Bees buzzing around the thousands of pink pinhead flowers on the spirea shrubs next to the porch. The rustle of the leaves from the breeze in the trees and the corn plants making their own music. The U.S. flag brushing against its own fabric in the wind. A car or two on the highway, the panting of Piper, my black German Shepard, and the crunch of some gravel underneath the tire of the bike that just went by. How sweet is that?

Smell. Take a deep breath through your nose. The fresh-cut alfalfa in the field behind the hill makes memories come flooding back. Love that smell. Love those memories. Today, I'm breathing in the pure and fresh country air, yet it feels stale from the humidity. It makes me think about the hazy days of unloading hay in the hot sun and wiping my brow with a hanky. There is beauty in all of it. The cycle of life is constant. Yet, the constant change brings the consistency that the world needs.

Relish in the moment. Something I'm learning to do more of. I have the above visual archived in my mind because I was mindful of some simple things. This is living in the moment. Relish it! Today is a gift, that's why they call it 'the present.' Presents come in all shapes and sizes. Moments bring one present after the other.

Life Lesson: Stop. Look. Listen. Smell. What present is awaiting you?

◆ ◆ ◆

ACRE 17

Life is good. . .
But only if you make it that way!

L et's face it—there are a lot of bad things hap-
pening in our world. From homelessness to
human trafficking to school shootings. Not
to mention the unethical politics that surround us.
Then, we turn to our own lives as we experience
job loss, hunger, disease, abuse, death, and even the
daily grind of getting up, showing up, and trying to
do what's right. How does one ignore all of that? We
don't. How can we stop it? We can't. But we can make
the world a better place with how we react to it.

I'm not a psychiatrist or a psychologist and I don't
want to downplay the fact that many have experienced physical and emotional scarring that I cannot
comprehend or even pretend to understand. There is
never just one solution or path, and we all must find
what works for ourselves and our experiences.

I have found that my life is a lot more fulfill-
ing when I let go of regret and anger and control.
I'm happiest when I'm learning and living with deep
gratitude for what I do have, and who I am. Life is

more enjoyable when I live through gratitude. I could spend my life regretting growing up on a farm. Regretting the work. Regretting not having summers off. Regretting the 'hardships' of only participating in one school event a year or wearing hand-me-down clothes, or not feeling I had the money or the worthiness to attend college. I could be angry over losing my job after 26 years at the place where I thought I would retire. I could be jealous of those who have more money or things or even more happiness than me.

As humans, we can place way too much emphasis on things. A simplistic example of this as I reflect on my childhood: If someone had told me when I was eight that it didn't matter whether my bike was new or a hand me down, I would not have believed them. Yet today, I can't recall if it was or not. But I can still feel the breeze in my hair and picture the yard I pedaled around and hear the sound of my shoe tips dragging to brake.

Life is about moments and experiences and relationships. When I make choices to be grateful, be joyful, and be mindful, and focus on what's right in the world, instead of what is wrong, I am happier. Because in the end, there are always more challenging times ahead.

This whole book is about experiences and relationships and living life to the fullest. I've shared a lot about what has shaped me and the lessons I've learned. I did not and do not always follow my own life lessons. I, too, am a work in progress.

I'll leave you with one final lesson: Never underestimate your power to make a difference to another. It wasn't until after my father passed away that I realized the impact he made through one small gesture. When I—or anyone—walked into a room, my father would look up, smile with that twinkle in his eye and say one simple word with enthusiasm. "Nancy!"

There are two kinds of people in this world. Those who walk into a room and say, "Here I am" and those who walk into a room and say, "There you are.""
—Ann Landers

Life Lesson: Be a "There you are!" sorta person. Spread joy!

I wish you peace and happiness.

❖ ❖ ❖

The Back Forty
—Summary of
Life Lessons

T hrough the thicket or around the bend. Unseen by passersby, yet sometimes found by a group of teenagers who want to party secretly, lies the 'Back Forty.' The term came from the Homestead Act, signed into law in 1862. Farmers were granted a quarter section of land. A full section was 640 acres, a quarter section was 160 acres, and the quarter section was itself subdivided into four quarter-quarter sections of 40 acres each: two *front forty* and two *back forty*.

When granted, the land may not have looked to be prime land. When cleared, it turned hillsides and prairie into fields to produce the necessary crops for the farm animals. The name is deceiving, as many believe it to be just 40 acres when it's actually 80.

Like the Back Forty, life lessons can be difficult to get to. They often come from painful experiences that we tuck in the back of our minds and pretend never happened. The joyful experiences offer equally valuable lessons, but are often forgotten as we are looking for the next best thing. The experiences and their lessons are a part of you, whether you want them to be or not. They make up your journey. Embrace them and you become your true, authentic self.

It is here, in my Back Forty acres, that I am placing my life lessons. Because they are difficult to uncover, can be painful to remember, and sometimes hard to accept. There is beauty once you uncover them and accept that they have shaped you. I have been blessed with our farm's Back Forty being adjacent to the land I purchased in 1995 from my parents. My father made it part of the land conservation and it will never be developed. I walked the Back Forty as I reflected and uncovered many of my own life lessons. This process has helped me live life! I believe that reflection is a key ingredient to acceptance. I am who I am through these life experiences. I own that. It is something no one can take away from me. It is something I choose to use to become the best version of myself. I hope you can find a place or space to reflect and uncover your life lessons—then put them to good use to change the world, or at least a corner of it.

Acre 1: True Love

- Hold tight to your dream. Where there is a will, there's a way.
- Find the courage to accept one another just the way you are.
- Respect, accept and encourage one another.

Acre 2: Zander Clan

- Resilience—push through and carry on.
- Prayer is powerful.
- Fight back. Learn to stand up for yourself.
- My sisters will be forever friends.
- Imagination is better than any toy you can purchase.
- Your decisions. Your outcomes. Choose wisely.
- Don't let disappointment or disagreement get in the way of a relationship.
- It's none of your business what others think of you. And, almost always, it's not about you.
- Venture courageously.
- Home is where the heart is. You are always welcomed home
- Believe in angels!

Acre 3: Through the Curtain

- The best things in life are free: love, hugs, kindness, patience, and imagination.
- Find what warms your heart.
- Save for what is needed and wait for what is wanted.
- We come into this world with family and leave the world with family. Take care of family.

Acre 4: School's out for SUMMER!

- Create an 'outta sight' space. Make time for

YOU.
- Be carefree! Free from worries, free from anxiety. Carefree is the best kind of FREE.
- When you work hard, you can rest easy.
- Nature is magical.
- A family that plays together, stays together.
- Appreciate the simple things in life.

Acre 5: Do-A-Dab

- Rise and shine—literally!
- Take educated risks—be innovative to grow your business.
- If you are going to do a job, do the job well. No halfsies.
- Take pride in your day's work.

Acre 6: Bringing the Cows Home

- Sing as if no one is listening.
- Pick a flower. Enjoy the view.
- Our life experiences—our stories—are unique and worthy of sharing.
- Get it while it's hot.

Acre 7: White Gold

- Quality work produces quality results.
- No matter what job you do, do it well.
- When in doubt, toss it out.
- Inflation does not ensure revenue.
- Farming is more than a livelihood, it's a life.

Acre 8: No Warning

- Things can be replaced. People cannot.
- Nature deserves our appreciation and respect.
- Protect your assets.
- Take responsibility, no matter what the obstacles are.
- When you get shit on, go spray it off!
- Be thankful when you escape the wrath of a storm, an illness, or an accident.

Acre 9: Give Back

- Be a hipster!
- If you are not early, you are late.
- Get involved!
- Keep your commitments.

Acre 10: The Scandal

- Honesty prevails.
- Financial agreements should be in writing.
- Perseverance.
- Rhubarb leaves are poisonous.
- Love prevails.

Acre 11: Decades and Milestones

- Love the ones you're with.
- Be quirky. It's 'food for the soul.'
- All that truly matters, in the end, is that you truly loved and were loved.

Acre 12: The Letter

- Stand up for your beliefs and educate others along the way.

- Make a difference.
- Write letters, especially love letters. Say "I love you."

Acre 13: An Auction

- Memories are more important than possessions.
- Change is inevitable. The only thing constant is change itself.

Acre 14: Life Changer

- *"To say good-bye is to die a little."*
- Be resilient.
- Be a life changer.

Acre 15: Ties that Bind

- Family is forever!

Acre 16: Relish in the Moment

- Learn to relish.
- Stop. Look. Listen. Smell. What present is awaiting you?

Acre 17: Life is Good . . . But only if you make it that way!

- Be a "There you are!" sorta person.
- Spread Joy!

www.ingramcontent.com/pod-product-compliance
Lightning Source LLC
LaVergne TN
LVHW051304080426
835509LV00020B/3142